SUCCESS WITH SUCCESSION

SUCCESS

—— WITH ——

SUCCESSION

How to Sell Your Asset Management
and Financial Advice Practice

PAUL FRANCO, CFP®

LIONCREST
PUBLISHING

SUCCESS WITH SUCCESSION

How to Sell Your Asset Management and Financial Advice Practice

FIRST EDITION

ISBN   978-1-5445-4502-8   *Paperback*
       978-1-5445-4501-1   *Ebook*

To all of the advisors who know it's time to begin creating your exit strategy—we are here to simplify your life so you can do more of what you love!

CONTENTS

INTRODUCTION

I RECENTLY STOPPED IN TO SEE AN OLD FRIEND WHO HAS a financial advisor practice in a midsize town about an hour south of my home in Colorado Springs. He's got a small office in the downtown area, and when I walked in, I found him reading the newspaper at his desk with the Golf Channel playing on the nearby television.

Later, as we strolled down the main street to a restaurant for lunch, my buddy waved to a couple of people passing by in cars and then paused to chat with a few others coming out of stores or heading into the bank. These were all clients or friends of his. It seemed like he knew everyone. At one point, I laughed and said, "You're practically the mayor of this town!" My friend nodded and smiled. We popped into the diner, and the hostess immediately took us back to my friend's "usual" table and brought him the drink he always orders. The mayor, indeed.

My friend is sixty-nine, and I asked him if he was giving any thought to retiring and selling his practice. I knew his practice would be desirable to many buyers, including me. I said, "You could do quite well," I told him. "You have a lot of recurring revenue, and that drives a pretty good price."

My friend admitted that he had thought about selling but had decided that he wasn't ready yet to take down his shingle. He'd worked many years to develop his practice, and now that it was producing good revenue, he wanted to continue working and earning. Most importantly, he had no idea how he would fill his time if he retired.

"What would I do with myself?" he asked me. "What would my clients do? They're happy to keep me around."

We had a pleasant lunch, and as I drove north on Interstate 25, I thought a lot about my friend's situation. Although he was a good financial advisor and had served his clients well over the years, I could see that his practice was starting to wind down. He was an old-school broker, selling financial products but not offering his clients comprehensive advice. He wasn't adopting the latest technology. He wasn't adding any new clients, and the average age of his clients was increasing. Most of them were even older than him, reaching the age when they start drawing down their portfolios rather than expanding them, and my friend seemed content to let his assets under management decline this way.

Unfortunately, my friend is missing an opportunity. The demand among financial advisors interested in buying retiring advisors' practices is stronger than ever. It is a seller's market. Many advisors have delayed retirement because their income is so good, but they have underestimated what their "book" is worth. Many have no idea what their practice is worth, and many have never gotten an independent third-party valuation of their practice to get an idea of how much they could get from a sale.

What's more, my friend probably isn't aware that many practice sales now are at least partially bank-financed, meaning that he could collect his payout at closing and retire with a nice nest egg—in his case, somewhere north of $2 million. His practice was his most valuable asset—something he'd spent decades building—but he couldn't bring himself to capitalize on it.

It also occurred to me that my friend was frittering away that asset.

About this time, I had lunch with another friend with a financial planning practice. He was approaching retirement differently. Instead of hanging on to a practice declining in value, he brought in a younger but experienced advisor to buy his practice. The new guy got financing from the Small Business Administration, and the two swapped places: my friend became the associate, and his young colleague took over as the primary financial planner for the practice. He plans to continue working for the next two years, using that time to prepare his clients for his retirement. He is still calling his favorites and servicing their accounts, and as a result, he expects very few will leave when he does finally retire. Many of his clients have started asking for consultations with the new guy. My friend is happy taking a back seat! He's only doing the type of work he enjoys, not the drudgery, and he's getting to spend more time at his future retirement home in Scottsdale, Arizona.

Most of us see the most significant growth in our asset management practices in our fifties and into our sixties. That's when our number of high-value and affluent clients is at its peak. Instead of the modest income we made from our younger, less-wealthy clients earlier in our career, we are now making a more rewarding income working with older, more prosperous clients. That's hard for many advisors to give up. They like that income. They worked for it. And it comes easily.

But by delaying their retirement, they miss an opportunity to sell their practice when it is at its highest valuation. As their clients age, the value of the advisor's practice declines steadily. The money the advisor loses by waiting too long to sell may not be recouped by the annual revenue they earn by staying on the job. The longer you wait, the less likely you'll be exiting the business on your terms rather than have it forced on you by external factors.

A complex study of more than 50,000 households revealed the point at which an advisor's client base reaches its peak based on the clients' average ages and the percentage of investors who are either basic (with below $100,000 in assets under management), high value ($100,000 to $500,000), or affluent ($500,000 or more in AUM). The analysis showed a strong correlation between the average age of your clients and the revenue growth of the advisor's practice. Revenue grows until the client reaches a certain age (sixty-three, typically), and then revenue declines. You can put the numbers from your practice through a computer model to determine when your practice is at its peak and worth the most to a potential practice buyer.

Here's an example. An advising practice with $1.39 million in annual revenue with a certain client segmentation would have a peak practice value of about $3 million in 2022. After that, as the clients age, the value declines steadily. If the advisor waited five years to sell and didn't add any new clients, annual revenue would be $1.33 million, and the practice value would be $2.8 million. If the advisor waited ten years, revenue would be $1.2 million, but the practice value would be just under $2.5 million. Waiting ten years would cost the advisor over a half-million dollars. But it's probably even more! There is another factor at work besides your clients spending down their money. Many of your clients start noticing that you're not as active in providing ongoing service, your advice isn't as concise and sharp as it used to be, and they vote with their feet. They move on to an advisor who is more engaged on their behalf.

I was sure my friend's ambivalence about retiring cost him that kind of money.

KNOWING WHEN TO SELL

Frankly, my friend's situation is not unusual. It's pretty common.

The average age of financial advisors in the United States is fifty-five, with approximately 38 percent planning to retire over the next ten years. Twenty percent of financial advisors are over age sixty-five! This means many are approaching the age when most professionals are planning retirement. Most financial advisors, however, hang on longer than they should, allowing their skills to get rusty and their service to clients to decline. Many fail to learn new practices or embrace modern technology, further eroding their effectiveness and ability to meet client expectations. Their practice loses value. By some estimates, they can lose 25–33 percent of their practice's value by delaying retirement.

And why do they delay? If you ask twenty different advisors, you'll get twenty different answers. But one common thread that runs through that discussion is this: many advisors don't realize the value of retiring at their practice's peak. They don't understand the different options for selling or that they can sell and continue to work, which is essentially the best of both worlds. It's also true that the financial planning profession is still relatively young. It's been just thirty-eight years since the Certified Financial Planner™ Board of Standards was created in 1985. Until recently, there hasn't been a template for how to retire.

As a result, many think selling a practice requires a lot of guesswork and risk. They think it's time consuming, emotionally challenging, or mysterious. But it's fairly easy.

The goal of this book is to erase some common misconceptions about selling your financial advising practice. I'll explain how to get a valuation of your practice, improve its value before selling, find a buyer who will continue the legacy you've built over the years, and communicate the transition to your clients with little or no attrition.

This book is also for advisors who are new to the industry or have experience but are still several years away from retirement. We'll talk about how you can ensure your practice is growing and gaining value and is protected in the face of unexpected misfortune. We'll show you how recruiting the right mix of clients over the age and wealth spectrum can set you up for a rewarding payday when it comes time to sell your practice.

Some of you close to retirement may be an employee advisor at one of the large wirehouse firms or one of the large broker-dealers. If you transition your practice to someone within your firm, you may only get a price equal to the recurring revenue of your clients. You may not get a choice of who your successor will be. What you'll learn in this book may convince you to leave your firm, join another for a few years, and then sell your book for two or three times the recurring value or even more.

I also hope some of you who are still early in your careers and working as sole practitioners will see value in this book. Many of you are drowning under the growing demands of regulatory paperwork, but your practice is not big enough to justify hiring someone to help. You're stuck, but I hope this book will show the value of joining a larger firm that's growing. In return for your assets, you get internal staff help and an opportunity to grow with the organization as it acquires more practices from retiring advisors.

Here are some other topics we'll cover:

- **Do you need a succession plan or an exit strategy?** Some advisors want to take time and groom their successors for a slow transition that's barely noticeable to their clients. Others are simply ready to sell right now on the open market. We'll explore these and other scenarios that might make sense to you.
- **Your practice's valuation.** What factors affect how much your book is valued, and does your valuation always determine your market price? Should you use the market approach for valuation or the income approach? What about using both?
- **Valuation drivers.** What characteristics drive up the value of a practice, and which ones drive it down? How often should you have a valuation done on your practice, and why should you consider it even if you're not planning to retire? How can you drive up your practice's value?
- **Choosing the right payout.** Do I want an income stream or a lump sum payment when I finalize the sale? What about stock? Should I switch firms before selling?
- **Case studies.** We'll look at several different sales and

analyze how the deals were structured, which ones did well, and which ones could have been better.

- **Making the deal.** What can you expect when you put your practice up for sale? How can you ensure you find the right buyer for your clients? How will you break the news to your investors?
- **Welcome to retirement.** You've made the sale, and it's time to wax your skis. Or is it? What will your ongoing obligations be? What are you going to do with your sales revenue? Do you need an advisor of your own?

WHY I'M WRITING THIS BOOK

As a financial advisor for more than twenty-eight years, I've been involved in buying and selling many practices. I've helped transition practices within my broker-dealer, and I've also worked on external sales. What I've learned is that each transaction is different. Each seller has unique needs, and each buyer comes with unique opportunities or challenges. I've expanded my practice through acquisition, but I've also helped others merge or complete sales.

What I've learned over the years is that most advisors have never taken the time to understand what it means to sell their practice. As a result, there are many misconceptions. Some assume they'll be able to control when they retire, but it's often decided for you by outside factors. Others think they're ready to retire and sell their practice today when the truth is they aren't and will be leaving money on the table if they leave today. If there is one universal truth, most advisors *overestimate* how much they'll make by continuing to work, and they *underestimate* how much their practice is worth.

I've seen what happens to those who hang on too long

without a succession plan or an exit strategy. Some get sick, and their spouses must come in and conduct a fire sale of the business they spent a lifetime building. Others fail to keep up with rapidly changing regulations, make mistakes, and get the boot or lose a key group of clients. Some stop doing any proactive service (if they ever did any in the first place) when client expectations for contact are higher than ever. They handle their clients' incoming calls and make transactions but do little to proactively advise their clients. Still others hang on until their rent goes up or a key employee quits, and they have no choice but to sell. The result is that they are forced to quit on someone else's terms, and that's never a happy ending.

This book is a simple, straightforward guide to avoiding those missteps and navigating smoothly through this pivotal period of your life. Retiring and selling your practice doesn't need to be a frightening uncertain time. Rather, it should be a rewarding time, a chance for you to fully appreciate all you've built and all the goodwill and trust you've engendered. This book will help you more fully enjoy that. Simply put, I want you to get the maximum price for your business with the least disruption and get out in a way that leaves your clients feeling good and allows you and your family to sail off into the sunset.

Your practice is probably the most significant asset you have. You shouldn't have to figure out how to find the best buyer at the best price entirely on your own. You need some help. We all do. We need help understanding the process and the best path through that process. Whereas buyers may have gone through the process several times, most sellers will go through it just once. We have one shot at getting it right. This book will ensure your aim is true.

One of the ironies of our profession is that even though we have built our careers on helping others prepare for a comfortable retirement, many of us are woefully unprepared for our own. We've failed to picture what life after work will be like. We've worked so hard for so long to convince people to trust us with their nest eggs that we've neglected to consider our own needs.

I hope this book will help us do a better job of that. There *is* a life after advising. Like my friend—the unofficial mayor of his town—you must make some adjustments. You may no longer dress in a suit every morning and greet your clients as you stroll down Main Street for lunch at your special table in the back. But selling your practice may enable you to enjoy other distinctions—the warm realization that your clients are in good hands, for instance, or that their children will now have another advisor to grow old with. Ultimately, my goal with this book is to help you enjoy the fruits of all the hard work you've put into your practice over the years.

You deserve it. You earned it.

1

READY TO RETIRE?

IT'S A QUESTION MANY OF US COULD STAND TO ASK OUR-selves: Am I ready to sell my practice?

A friend of mine—we'll call him Robert—was certain his answer was a resounding no. Like many successful, hard-working financial advisors, Robert had spent decades establishing a practice that produced consistent revenues. He rarely felt the need to take proactive steps to improve his practice. The practice seemed to grow organically, with referrals here and there that increased the value of his practice. His client base seemed secure, with no signs of attrition, so he felt little need to adopt the latest technology or customer-engagement trends. Indeed, Robert had reached what some might call the "golden years" of advising—when his business was so well established, he could afford to quit chasing new clients, reduce his working hours, and let those hard-earned dollars roll in. There was, he believed, no reason to consider selling his book.

Unfortunately, he was wrong.

A bit of a lone wolf, Robert worked as a solo advisor supported by a part-time administrative assistant. As he settled more and more comfortably into his low-pressure position, Robert failed to keep abreast of regulatory developments, and it cost him. He failed to follow regulations in some instances. He was supposed to confirm all trades with his clients but often didn't. One client had trouble reading her monthly statement and rather than spend time explaining it to her, Robert changed the address on her statement and had it delivered to him at his office instead. Yikes! Somehow this didn't get him fired. In time, Robert lost clients, and the value of his practice declined. He lost the trust and respect of his clients and put himself in jeopardy with his firm.

Robert's late-career sloppiness with legal and ethical standards would have been damaging enough. But he'd also failed to adapt to a significant trend in financial planning: the expectation that advisors will keep in frequent contact with their clients.

Like Robert, many financial advisors—especially those who've worked in this field for decades—still live by the old model of meeting new clients once, establishing their financial goals and approaches, and then only reaching out again to sell a fresh financial product. Simply put, this model no longer works. Clients expect their financial advisors to stay in touch, keep their unique needs and goals in mind, and watch the market for relevant opportunities. Financial advisors must be prepared to advise on insurance, estate planning, education costs, and tax strategies—not just invest-ment advice. There is a strong preference for fee-based comprehensive planning. More and more practices now offer clients ways to interact directly with their financial planning: internet portals that allow clients to check on their portfolios, regular email updates on any significant changes in the market, and more. They have to provide something more than an investor can read in an article on Investopedia. Naturally, forward-thinking practices that offer these services eagerly advertise their benefits, so underserved clients are fully aware that they are missing out.

This is what happened to my friend Robert. Already undermined by his regulatory issues, he began losing clients to practices that served their people more proactively. His book rapidly lost value, his revenues dipped, and Robert soon realized that selling his practice was no longer just a choice—it was the only option.

Business, like life, is unpredictable. By the time Robert could sell, his practice had decreased in value by about 40 percent. Rather than retiring when it was most profitable—and on his terms—Robert was forced out of the market to avoid taking even heavier losses.

WHAT ARE SOME SIGNS THAT IT MIGHT BE A GOOD TIME TO RETIRE?

Clients today hold you to a much higher standard of service. It's no longer good enough to respond to a call or email later in the week. The expectation is to return client contact the same day. Many experts will say that clients are expecting responses within two hours! Frequency of contact is also key. Clients expect at least four proactive meetings or contacts from you annually. Your clients are also much less tolerant of you or your team's errors.

With Robert's experience in mind, let's ask ourselves again, *Am I ready to sell my practice?* To flesh out your answer, consider a few additional questions.

Have you begun taking a less proactive approach to meeting your clients' needs?

Are you adding value above and beyond just investment advice? You had better be doing comprehensive planning or at least giving comprehensive advice. The investment portion of our industry has become commoditized—clients can get that from anyone or even with online tools. You have to offer more. Clients expect you to give them help on the questions they can't readily find out themselves—Am I okay for retirement? Are my kids going to be able to go to college? Am I still on track with this market drop? Most importantly, they are looking for peace of mind.

Our longtime clients tend to be forgiving of our quirks and foibles. However, you must not underestimate the expectation today that you get back to your clients quickly. Your clients expect a fast response and are much less forgiving of you taking your time to get back to them and answer their questions.

The industry is changing, with new technology introduced every day. If you aren't embracing these changes—offering online meetings, digital presentations, video conferences, paperless offices, and more—it might be a good time to sell. Do you take an active interest in the market, keeping abreast of service trends and client expectations? Or are you uninterested in learning new technologies and altering your approach? If the latter sounds like you, you might consider retiring before the market evolves right past you.

Your clients expect you to be technologically adept, and they expect you to be using the latest tools. They expect a full multimedia presentation, presented on their terms—whether they prefer to meet in the office, access content on their phone while they are out hiking, or on their TV at home. The days when a meeting only meant coming to an office, sitting at a chair next to the advisor's big desk, and leaving with a printout of your accounts are over.

Investors expect a first-rate online experience. You need to have an excellent website. One pathetic trend I've found is independent advisors buying their website templates from a standard provider. The content and look of their website are the same as other advisors. Only the advisor and practice name are different! And yet I've heard advisors with these templated websites tell me how proud they are of their "customized website."

Clients also expect many other online tools. Can they easily find their balances and investment returns? What if they want to access a copy of last year's tax statement? Can they make simple money movement transactions themselves? Deposit a check into their account using their cell phone?

A common mistake advisors make is to assume "my clients don't care about technology." Even your little old lady clients are using Zoom to visit with their grandkids. Ignore the technological enhancements to the service process at your peril.

Are you keeping up with changes to regulatory requirements?

Many financial advisors—especially those running a one-advisor show—have found recent regulatory changes overwhelming. Perhaps you've fallen behind on paperwork or have failed to adjust your business practices. If the growing regulatory burden is consuming your hours, that could be another sign that you should leave. A common comment from advisors is, "I have so many great opportunities, but the paperwork is killing me. If I had the right people around me, I could go out and grow my book."

It's reached the point where the paperwork required to

satisfy your firm and the regulators makes it very difficult to continue as a "lone wolf" advisor. We are increasingly seeing advisors band together in large team practices as a response to the complexity of our business.

Has your practice peaked?

As Robert learned, the best time to sell your practice is when your book is at its most valuable—when your clients are producing solid revenues, assets are growing, and your client base is strong and diverse. You have good communication practices that potential buyers can adopt and continue without missing a beat. It might feel counterproductive to carefully scale that business development hill just to sell once you reach the crest, but this is the moment when your ROI will be at its highest. Why not take advantage?

WHY DO SOME ADVISORS CHOOSE TO DELAY RETIREMENT?

Over the years, I've met with dozens of advisors to gauge their interest in selling. Some tell me they keep working out of loyalty to their clients. But in meeting after meeting, the two major motivators I hear for saying no to a potential sale are comfort and fear.

Like my friend Robert, many advisors have no interest in retirement because they're comfortable where they are. Donning a nice suit, going to the office, and making the occasional client appointment gives them a sense of purpose—and they appreciate the security of ongoing revenue. The money comes so easily, so why would you walk away from it? In my meetings with advisors, it's not until I walk them through some quick napkin math that they realize that selling now could be more profitable long term than maintaining a business on the road to decay.

At this point, many advisors shake off that cozy comfort and leave our meetings feeling invigorated at the prospect of selling while the selling's good. However, by the time our second meeting rolls around a few weeks later, that second motivator has often taken root: fear. Consistent income is like a favorite old blanket, warm and reassuring, and they worry that losing it could leave them shivering in a cold and uncertain retirement. Here's another way to look at it. Say you draw a nice hot bath and settle in for a long soak. But after a while, the water temperature drops, and you start to feel cool. But you stay in the water because getting out means getting colder. So you continue to sit.

But as you consider your options, remember that retirement can look much more affordable if you suddenly have an extra few million in your pocket. How would that kind of money change your outlook on your retirement years? What avenues could open in terms of debt payoff, investment, savings, and the opportunity to more fully and freely enjoy your life?

WHY SELL NOW SPECIFICALLY?

I'll give you three reasons: market scarcity, personal legacy, and client satisfaction. A roaring stock market makes your practice worth more than ever.

We are currently in the midst of a seller's market. Many advisors have put off retiring, creating a scarcity of available books and driving up their value. However, this state can't last forever. If many advisors were to retire at once, this resulting glut of available practices would drive down the value of your book. Why not consider selling now when the market is hot?

Just as importantly, if you proactively plan your retirement and the sale of your business, you can ensure that your legacy—the culmination of your decades of work—is preserved. How likely is your practice to outlive you if some unforeseen mishap or expense forces you prematurely from the market? In that case, your practice will not go to a carefully selected successor but to the highest bidder. You will have little say in who acquires your business and clients.

If you develop a specific succession plan, you can personally identify the next generation of talent: a trusted partner or vigorous newcomer who'll serve your clients with the same care they expect from you. You can repay your clients' trust with a smooth transition, unbroken service, and peace of mind. After all, this is their financial future, so why not do what you do best, and plan for their security?

While writing this book, the stock market took a hopefully brief but steep dive. When that happens, the value of your book will decline. If you were selling during that period, your practice valuation probably dropped. If you were acquiring practices, the downturn made it a good time to buy.

But even during that downturn, we didn't see practice sale activity decline noticeably. Financial advisors understand that bear markets are inevitable but that it's rarely a long-term situation. The market always comes back. Still, for sellers, the timing is essential.

EXIT STRATEGY—CREATING AN EMERGENCY TRANSITION PLAN

Even if you're just starting to build your book and are not close to retiring, it's wise to have an exit strategy.

An exit strategy should include a death and disability agreement with another advisor. If you die or cannot work, your practice transitions to the other advisor. That death or disability agreement is something you can put in place at any time, and everyone should have one. If you don't have one and become disabled, you could stand to lose your practice. Make a plan.

Some industry experts call these death and disability agreements "continuity plans." In this book, a continuity plan refers to your plan for transferring your business operations—leases, staff, vendors, and so forth—to a buyer. For our purposes, we'll refer to these death and disability plans as "emergency transition plans."

Emergency transition plans assure the easy transfer of control and responsibility of your practice when you suddenly depart—either through death, illness, termination, partner disputes, or whim (such as when you decide to immediately go on that three-year motorcycle trip to Tierra del Fuego). Usually, this emergency transition plan is a subset of your formal succession plan and it only comes into play for sudden, unexpected developments.

Most financial planners don't start thinking about succession plans until they are fifty or so, but you should have a transition plan in place as soon as the size of your practice warrants it. Here are some quick tips for preparing your emergency transition plan:

- Detail what constitutes the emergency: death, illness, loss of license, and so forth.
- Identify how your practice will be valued at the time of the transition. Simple

valuation by a third party? Simple formula based on assets under management?

- Establish the payment terms.
- Identify the buyer.
- Identify a third-party "executor" for the deal if your firm or partners decide not to step forward to execute the transition.
- Supply a continuity plan for your successors. This plan should set out your office's practices and procedures, client management software, and other details that allow your successor to step in quickly and keep the office running smoothly.

These emergency transition plans should be continually reviewed and updated as your situation changes. You may want to schedule an annually recurring valuation of your practice. That provides a track record of the growth of your practice over time and can reduce disagreements about its value in the event something unexpected happens.

An acquaintance recently shared that he's fighting a genetic disorder that is slowly eroding his mobility and speech. He knows this condition will put him out of business sooner rather than later, so he's been eager to find a successor. If this friend had begun his search ten years ago, this diagnosis would be less of a problem now; the succession plan would already be established, and the successor would already be learning his system and clients. The problem is that this acquaintance is already fifty-nine—a common retirement age even without a disabling condition. As much as he might hate selling his carefully crafted business, finding and training a suitable successor could easily take half a decade or more. Not everyone has that kind of time.

KEY TAKEAWAY

Maybe you're not ready to retire, but maybe your practice is. It's time to consider where you are on that business development hill—still climbing, at your peak, or already coasting down the other side—and act if the moment is right. If you wait until you're ready, then, like my friend Robert, you could end up forced out of the market, leaving piles of money on the table. You built this business, so you deserve to put that money where it belongs—in your pocket.

Before you take the critical step of selling, however, you might want to do a few things to make the sale more lucrative. Let's move on to the next chapter and find out how to do that.

2

IMPROVING YOUR PRACTICE'S VALUE

YOU'VE PROBABLY FELT THE LURE OF A QUICK COMMISSION. A friend calls it "the quick, cocaine-like hit of getting a bunch of money all at once."

Let's say you're working with a client and an annuity is a great fit for her situation. You and the client agree to put $400,000 into the annuity. Taking the compensation up front might generate a commission of $20,000 or even more!

"Wow," you think, "I could put that money right into my mortgage. I could pay off my car." But as appealing as that lump sum looks, you will never earn another nickel on this large amount of money. Worse, it adds nothing to your long-term practice sales value.

In other words, sometimes it pays to ignore that short-term win and take the long view. Take the 1 percent trailing compensation on this annuity, and you'll be paid on it year after year.

But what does this have to do with selling your business?

When considering books for sale, buyers search for specific, appealing characteristics—details that say your practice is not just a good investment but an easy one. Do you have great recurring revenue? Do you have enough younger clients to balance out the older ones? Do you have a system for keeping clients engaged? Is there a business continuity plan in place?

If you answered no to any of these questions, keep this in mind: Making any of these improvements to your practice is possible—but not at the last minute. So instead of leaping right into your sale, take a few minutes to consider the long view. How could you raise the value of your business over the next six months? Nine months? A year?

WORK ON YOUR BOOK

People like easy. So if you can turn your business into an easy investment with high returns and little extra legwork, the number of interested buyers will shoot up. What follows are some steps you can take to achieve that.

SHAVE OFF SMALL-TIME CLIENTS

Letting any client go might sound counterintuitive, especially if they're bringing in revenue. But as we discussed in the last chapter, it takes as much effort to support a client with $10,000 as a client with $10 million. So to show buyers that your books will bring them a good ROI—without a ton of additional work—try trimming out some of your lowest earners.

What might this look like? When the COVID-19 pandemic first hit, my partners and I surveyed the changing landscape and thought we were in trouble. The market, we believed, was about to drop and drop hard. We didn't feel we would be able to serve everyone at the high standard our clients have come to expect. So as a team, we decided to slim down our books—pruning out smaller-value clients we'd hoped would grow over time—to preserve the business.

I later shared this experience with a fellow advisor, who reacted with shock. "I could never just cut people out," he told me. "I live in a small town. I see these people all the time, I know them, and I can't just turn them over to another advisor or a home office call center. They'd hate me for it."

Indeed, it might sound self-serving, leaving smaller clients out in the cold for your financial gain. But as another advisor friend pointed out, you can design this transition to benefit the client just as much as yourself.

"It's the easiest thing in the world," this friend explained. "I go to my people and say, 'Look, I suggest you set up an account at Fidelity or Vanguard. You'll eliminate account maintenance fees that may be as much as $250 per year. Your costs to invest will be less. It'll save you a bunch of money. It's much more in your interest to have your finances over there.' And then they leave, saying, 'Thank you,' to me."

You care about your clients, so think of this move not as trimming the fat but as finding your lower-value clients a new and better home. Pick a figure—in my practice, it was clients who represented the bottom 10 percent in terms of assets under management—and see how they could benefit from moving on. Also, find a new home for what we call "time vampires"—clients who bring in little income but steal an excessive amount of your time.

A common mistake advisors make when thinking about

handing off clients is to say, "Well, I know Mrs. McGillicuddy only has $18,000 with us, but she doesn't require much from us either." WRONG. Even if you never talk to her, you have firm-level due diligence and regulatory requirements for her. When she passes away, the estate settlement may take your team hours to complete. You literally can't even *think* about her without losing money.

Repeat this process every single year.

GET CLIENTS OUT OF BROKERAGE AND INTO MANAGED ACCOUNTS

There's no question that recurring revenues beat the commission model over time. This is why so many advisors are moving toward 90 or even 95 percent of their revenue coming from managed accounts, which don't pay commissions but generate fees of around 1–2 percent of assets under management on an annual recurring basis. Anyone who does otherwise is just selling themselves short—especially when it comes to the sale of their practice. As I've mentioned, accounts with recurring revenue typically go for 2.5 times or more of their annual revenue. But if you take your money up front with a standard brokerage account—and never make that transition to managed—that 2.5x figure disappears, and you may not get anything when you sell your business.

I recently saw a practice for sale with $100 million in assets under management but only $250,000 in recurring revenue. If its owner were smart, they would have spent the years before the sale going through every single client, looking for those who would benefit from moving to a managed account. These typically are more sophisticated clients with more knowledge of investing. They often prefer to pay an asset-based fee versus commissions, prefer active portfolio management over passive management, and appreciate ongoing advice on when to buy and when to rebalance.

Many advisors have an aversion to charging an ongoing management fee. They believe that the client should pay an up-front commission once. After all, it is less expensive for the client over time. Consider some of the strengths of a managed account where the client pays an ongoing fee:

- In a managed account, you generally take a more active approach, and you'll be able to react more quickly to changing market conditions.
- A managed account aligns your interests and the client's interests. You both want to see the portfolio grow.
- With a managed account, the client doesn't question the underlying motives of your buy and sell recommendations because you aren't generating a new commission with each recommendation.
- A managed account provides a great incentive to the advisor to provide excellent service. If the client isn't happy with paying 1 percent on an ongoing basis to you, they can switch that account to another place with a bit of time and a few online signatures.
- Your clients need ongoing advice! It's a fact that the average investor earns far less than the market as a whole. They need your advice on an ongoing basis to keep them from making emotional decisions that hurt their portfolio.

Of course, a managed account isn't the solution for everyone in every case, but if you are a commission-based advisor, you must consider the benefits where it makes sense.

The last thing buyers want is a moldering book filled with old people and declining revenue. How can you keep yours fresh?

Start by evaluating the average age of your client base. Buyers know that client assets usually peak before retirement and decrease steadily after age seventy. To keep buyers interested, set up generational planning opportunities with clients' children and grandchildren. If you can sign the younger generations, this mitigates the risk to the buyer.

If you're an older advisor who is not marketing your business and replacing your older clients with younger investors, you sound the death knell for your book. On average, financial planners lose about 2.5–5 percent of their assets under management annually, so it's wise to remain proactive about servicing your existing clients and bringing new clients into the fold. Even if you aren't engaging with your clients regularly, you have to assume they are talking to other financial planners. And one of the first things that will come up in their conversation with your client is, "How often is your current planner communicating with you?"

Not sure how to bring in younger clients when you are an older curmudgeon and don't know any young people? Again, engage with the children of your older clients. Your older clients want their kids to have as few headaches as possible when they pass away. One of their children is usually the personal representative of their estate. There are many obvious benefits to including the children in an annual service meeting: they are aware of what Mom and Dad have, where the estate is invested, and potential problems. If you engage the children, there is a good chance that they will become your clients one day.

IMPROVE YOUR CLIENT ENGAGEMENT

A few years ago, I acquired a book from an advisor I'll call Leo. As I began reaching out to my new clients, I asked when they'd last spoken to him. "Oh, about ten years ago," they'd say, "when he sold me this annuity." And then directly after: "Why do you want me to come in for an appointment again? What would we even talk about?"

Leo was engaging in an old-fashioned client interaction model—no client interaction. This approach will no longer fly (if it ever did in the first place). If you aren't actively engaged with your clients and making proactive contact, they have a much higher probability of leaving you for greener pastures. This also applies to the tools you and your firm provide for them. Clients expect to engage with you and their money online through your website and your firm's portal. If there isn't a robust online presence, you can expect your clients to go elsewhere.

Do you have systems in place to stay in touch with your clients? You need, at a minimum, to segment your clients by the level of service you intend to provide for them. You should be able to demonstrate to your buyer that you are scheduling and seeing your clients regularly. For example, you might categorize some of your clients as "Gold," which means you see them in person twice a year and you reach out with a phone call or email two more times per year.

And let's be clear: you may have grown up in the days when seeing clients once a year was considered acceptable in this industry. It isn't today, and if this is your model, your practice is much less desirable to a buyer.

Being more proactive increases the health of your book and makes it more appealing to potential buyers. It's also more fun. When you are indispensable to your clients, they're happy, you feel good, and you get more referrals. Keeping clients in the fold is part of your job. Whereas investment recommendations are commoditized and financial planning software is commoditized, great comprehensive advice and conversations that go with that advice are not and never will be. That's what you provide, and that's what makes you valuable. Many old-timers still focus on providing simple investment advice, but that approach is going the way of the dodo.

So if you haven't already, consider what systems you can implement to engage clients predictably and effectively. Are you holding client appreciation events? Are you conducting online marketing to ensure that your practice continues to grow? Are you delivering a referrable client experience? Can your clients count on hearing from you two to four times a year?

Sure, buyers expect some attrition following a sale. But if you establish a client engagement system that can reduce those risks, buyers will view you as a much safer bet and make much stronger offers.

Your buyer also pays for the goodwill you've established over the years. They will want to know how well networked you are. What charities does your business support? What local civic organizations do you belong to? Do you give your employees time off to volunteer? Which Little League team do you sponsor, and what logo do you put on those uniforms?

MAKE YOUR BUSINESS EASY TO MANAGE

Track future business opportunities with your clients. A detailed opportunity list communicates that your clients have more growing to do, incentivizing buyers to pay a premium for your book. Do you have a systematized way of keeping track of the opportunities in your book? It could be as simple as a spreadsheet showing the client's name, a description of the opportunity, the estimated revenue from the opportunity, and the approximate date the opportunity can be realized.

As important as recurring revenue is, buyers most often acquire more than just your clients—they also take on the operations of your business. So if you want to increase your appeal, ask this question: *How can I make my business easier to run?*

LIST EVERYTHING

Instead of forcing buyers to dig through your files, develop itemized records of your business's day-to-day needs. Ensure to include ongoing expenses, such as the office lease, staff compensation, and marketing commitments. Also, note the names, contact information, and terms of engagement for any services currently supporting your business, including subscriptions, vendors, internet and phone, and technical support. And don't forget to protect your employees with an organization chart and detailed list of each staff member's duties, background, and desired career path, as well as any quirks or tips for retention that might come in handy for a new owner.

ESTABLISH A CONTINUITY PLAN FOR YOUR OFFICE

When you sell your practice, you are also likely selling your furniture, the lease, the equipment, and all the great people who work for you. To make that process seamless, you need a continuity plan that tells your buyer how many bills you have each month, how those bills are paid, how old your computers are, and what kind of IT agreement you have with contractors to keep them safe and current. A continuity plan lays out exactly what a buyer needs to know to keep your office running smoothly.

WORK OUT YOUR STORY AND COMMUNICATE YOUR VISION

Another way to pique buyers' interest is to deliver a focused, compelling story about your practice. Why did you get into this business in the first place? What kinds of clients do you most like to serve? Why do they come to you? What services, systems, or mission statement makes your practice special and worth acquiring? What is your value proposition to your clients and the buyer of your practice?

I sometimes sit down with advisors interested in selling, ask them these types of questions, and get a distinct impression that they're winging it. On the first pass, they'll give me one set of answers: "Oh, I have the best system for interacting with my clients. I focus primarily on female entrepreneurs and reach out to them at least twice a year." But by our second conversation, their story has often changed: "My favorite clients are high-value engineers, especially those nearing retirement. I reach out to them for a face-to-face chat quarterly." By the third conversation, they've gotten to know me better, and I often hear something like, "The truth is, I never really took the time to develop a target market, and for that matter, I don't have a very good system for keeping track of how I'm servicing my clients!"

If you're not clear on whom you serve and why—on what you're doing in this field—potential buyers will know it. So take the time to land on the who and why that power your business. Then use these details to build a focused, compelling story for which buyers will be willing to spend a premium. A great story resonates with your potential buyers. It makes you memorable and indicates a practice that is a better-than-average opportunity.

KEY TAKEAWAYS

How soon do you intend to sell? In five years? Three? The changes listed in this chapter can be accomplished in as little as one, so rather than jumping into a sale—taking that easy commission—slow down and take the long view. If you put in a little extra elbow grease, you might be surprised at the profits you can reap.

And once you're ready to accept those profits, consider your next big question: What kind of transition works best for me? Do I want to exit the business immediately? Or would it make sense to set up a succession plan and ease into retirement? Read on to learn how to best make that decision.

3

SALE OR SUCCESSION?

EVENTUALLY, WE'LL ALL PART WAYS WITH OUR CAREFULLY built businesses. And when that day comes, there are two words none of us wants to hear: fire sale.

Whether retirement is galloping at you fast or lingering on some distant horizon, how much control do you have over its timing? Any number of events could hasten its coming: an unforeseen medical diagnosis, the death of a family member, or the need to pick up your family and relocate to a new city. If you were to experience a medical emergency that resulted in your death or disability—and you had no plan—your departure would quickly diminish the value of your practice. Even worse, your grieving spouse could be left to pick up the pieces of your business, attempting to sell it without your help. A single emergency could force you to shut those doors, take down that sign, and arrange a quick and desperate sale—or be stuck with no sale.

The "fire sale" scenario wouldn't serve anyone (other than the advisors who picked up your book on the cheap). You and your beneficiaries would lose out on revenue. Your spouse could be forced to shoulder stressful business affairs.

Your clients would be shunted to an unfamiliar advisor with methods and character they've no reason to trust. And it would even reflect badly on others in our field, because who wants an advisor to map out their future if we don't even have the foresight to map out our own?

So before the unexpected can occur, start drawing out that map. I'll even hand you an easy way to begin.

In my experience, the most common methods of transferring ownership of your practice are a succession plan or an exit strategy. Essentially, a succession plan involves identifying someone to take over your practice, then working alongside them during a gradual transition spanning three to five years. On the other hand, an exit strategy is more of a straightforward sale. It involves finding a buyer, landing on a price you're happy with, then transferring ownership more rapidly, often within a year or so.

The right path for you depends on various factors, but the most immediate is generally time. At this point in your career, can you afford to take a more gradual, focused approach to finding a successor? Or are you ready—and just as importantly, is your practice ready—to sell off and get out of Dodge?

SUCCESSION PLAN

If you have the time and inclination to develop a succession plan, I can recommend several approaches to find your successor, all of which I'll discuss below. Each depends on the specific needs of your business as well as the availability of suitable "you" replacements.

TRANSFERRING TO A PARTNER

Do you work alone, or are there multiple advisors at your practice? If the latter, you might have a successor right under your nose. I'm fortunate to work alongside two talented advisors whose ages and experience make them ideal successors. Both are around forty years old and have learned the ropes. They've worked with my practice for several years and are familiar with all our systems, clients, and expectations. For the last several years, we've had an agreement in place that if I die, become disabled, or opt to retire, they will be my buyers, providing the smoothest and least complicated transition for all involved.

Perhaps you, like me, are lucky enough to work with talented, experienced, and relatively young advisors ready to take care of your clients when that day comes. If, however, you've more of a "lone wolf" setup, you might want to consider some other options.

HIRING A PARTNER

If you are early enough in your career, you might consider hiring a partner. In this case, you'd bring another experienced advisor into your firm on the partner level, then give them a year or two to learn the ins and outs of your particular practice.

The approach creates economies of scale and specialization. For example, we recently hired a financial advisor who previously worked as an engineer and has a strong background in project management. He understood the value of clear processes and procedures. He knew how to establish useful and efficient procedures. This appealed to us because none of us were as skilled in that area, and we felt his skills would complement ours. At the same time, we had expertise in areas where he was not as strong, and he felt he could learn a lot from us.

It makes your practice more valuable when you have people with complementary strengths. Working together requires teamwork and humility, but bringing in partners who add new skills to your team makes sense.

HIRING AN ASSOCIATE

You also have the option of bringing on an associate. An associate is usually a younger person who may never be a partner but has a smaller book and wants to be with a firm that will help them grow. Young hires are often ambitious, driven, and flexible, all of which can go a long way toward boosting your business. They are being groomed as a potential successor, and it's your job to give them the experience they need to reach their potential.

However, experience has taught me that young hires can also be flighty and unpredictable. I recently had lunch with a friend in his sixties seeking a successor. He described his experience of taking a chance on a young man fresh from college. "I hired him. I got him licensed. And just a week after he completed his licenses, later, he left me a voice mail saying he was quitting. I never heard from him again."

This series of events doesn't reflect well on the new hire. But to be fair to this young man, I know my friend well, and after decades as an advisor, he's a bit set in his ways. Worse, he would be a terrible coach to a new advisor. In a business where you have to be adaptable and open-minded, this friend has refused to embrace new technologies and client service systems for years. No new hire wants to work with a stagnant practice. They want to learn all the new technologies. If you've failed to bring modern practices to your business, hiring and training a younger associate might not be the right track. You may be highly skilled at talking to clients and making difficult concepts easy to understand, but training others is a much different skillset. An associate will expect systematic training, and most advisors at retirement age learned through trial and error and gutting it out. Most simply don't have any expertise in training someone. What's more, associates want a 401(k) and health insurance. Are you a great manager and trainer? Are you prepared to compete with larger firms that offer all these benefits?

You likely do not have the skillset to effectively hire, train, and mentor an advisor for your practice, no matter what your ego tells you. Your outdated, old-school ways of doing business will not appeal to a young go-getter.

SWITCHING TO YOUR SUCCESSOR'S FIRM

Another common approach is to move your business to a new practice at another firm and then find your successor among its advisors. You might feel resistant to shading your book under someone else's umbrella. Still, I've heard at least three compelling reasons financial advisors choose to do so: client welfare, financial strength, and ethical concerns.

First, let's consider client welfare. Imagine a broker living in my home state of Colorado. He knows who the potential buyers are at his current firm and doesn't feel good about his options. He may not even have a choice on who his successor will be—the firm may decide that for him. He's concerned that such organizations won't service his clients with the individual attention they expect or that their advice won't be tailored to their specific, local needs. So instead of selling to another practice at his current broker-dealer, this advisor chooses to join a local firm with an advisor who shares his values about how a client should be served. Gradually, he will move his clients into their more attentive care.

Second, consider that many advisors already operate as employees under the umbrella of massive firms but might not want to sell their books within those organizations. Many of these firms are notorious for only offering departing advisors a lesser buyout value than what they would receive in the independent world—the value of their recurring revenue, nothing more. An advisor may make two to three times as much selling externally, and they have more control over how their clients are transitioned.

Last, many advisors have found it prudent to transfer away from large firms where ethical violations have come to light in recent years. An advisor friend took steps to leave a large bank advisory firm after myriad violations were exposed there. Because this friend intends to retire within the next decade, he's carefully evaluating which advisors best suit each of his clients. He plans to slowly taper off his involvement with each client over the next three to five years once he's confident they're in good hands.

FINDING A BUYER

If you or your practice has reached the point where a quick sale to an external buyer looks like the best option, you're undoubtedly wondering how to find a suitable buyer. Sometimes that suitable buyer is a colleague or a friend in the business. Since my firm is actively interested in buying practices, I spend a lot of my time networking with advisors, discussing their transition plans, and describing how it makes sense for them to join our firm and sell to us when they retire. When it comes time for them to retire, I want them to think of me as a suitable buyer.

You can also sign up with a firm that sells financial planning practices. They will help you determine the value of your practice and then put it into the marketplace and vet potential buyers for you. We'll talk more about this type of sale in Chapter 7 when we discuss how firms are bought and sold in more detail.

INTERNAL SALES

Internal sales offer several advantages to consider. From a logistics standpoint, it's much easier to manage an internal sale since you and your buyer both belong to the same practice, business, or firm. Instead of going through the process of moving all your clients, all you have to do is get approval from your broker-dealer, fill out a single form, and by the next morning, all of your clients are listed under your new owner's name.

Remember that there are multiple types of internal sales:

- Bring in a young advisor, help them get licensed, and groom them to be an advisor.
- Bring in a family member, train them to get them licensed, and groom them to take over your practice.
- Sell to an experienced advisor on your team or at your firm.

Sometimes internal sales have some wrinkles that may

make them less desirable than external sales. For example, one company recently changed its policy regarding equity transfers. If you're doing an equity transfer within the company, they will charge the acquiring advisor 50 percent of the difference between the payout levels. For example, if the seller gets a payout of 72 percent and the buying practice has a 90 percent payout, the buyer has to pay 50 percent of that 18 percent difference.

In one case we're working on, our seller gets a 72 percent payout. In other words, if he sells an insurance policy for $100, he gets $72 of that sale and his firm gets 28 percent. But my team gets a 90 percent payout. If we acquire that seller's business, our parent firm's cut of those payouts drops from 28 percent to 10 percent. Our parent firm doesn't want that, so it's changing its policy. It will charge the acquiring advisor 50 percent of that lost business over three years to reduce that loss.

These policies may be an effective haircut of $100,000 or more! Even though the cost is charged to the buyer, understand that you, the seller, are ultimately paying this cost with a lowered practice purchase price.

EXTERNAL SALES

External sales **to an advisor at another firm** can be a little more involved. You will likely have to gain approval and do the transfer paperwork for each client individually. You'll almost certainly land a higher price if you go with an external buyer. External sales typically yield 2.5 to 3 times the AUM and sometimes even higher.

In a **closed sale**, a buyer and seller identify each other and work together to reach a deal. Think of this as based on a great relationship with another advisor colleague at another firm.

In an **open-market sale**, a professional broker manages the entire process on behalf of the seller, from accepting bids to vetting buyers. Generally speaking, open-market competition tends to drive up the cost of a practice, so of all three sales approaches, this one tends to produce the highest returns for sellers, even after the broker's percentage is factored in.

A major decision like this deserves careful deliberation, so if you're planning to sell, I'd recommend Chapters 3, 4, and 7 for more guidance on valuing your practice, making your business more attractive to buyers, and finalizing your deal.

DOES A MERGER MAKE SENSE?

If your operation is less a job and more of a practice, you might consider merging your entire business with someone else's.

The biggest advantage of mergers is the economies of scale. Smaller practices can join a larger team with specialists who can help the newcomer grow. When there is some synergy, one plus one can equal three. That's why large practices are becoming more common. Your payout from the merger will depend on the size of your book.

In a merger with a larger, more diversified team, you may also find that you can focus on the work you love and find someone else to do the work you don't care for. For example, you probably will be able to hand off a lot of your clerical work to a shared staff person who enjoys that sort of thing. Larger firms often supply health insurance, profit-sharing, and 401(k) matching funds—something you don't usually have in a smaller office. Joining a larger team also gives you people to bounce ideas off, share frustrations with, and tell war stories to. You get to work with and celebrate with like-minded people. Clients like it, too—it's nice to think a team of experts is watching over their money.

However, I have a word of caution regarding the merger approach. It's sometimes hard to tell if the people in your new firm truly share your values. You also have to accept that you are no longer the big cheese; you may have to set your ego aside after the merger, which can be challenging for some planners who are used to doing things their way. You may also have to learn new systems, practices, and standards in a merger. Those new rules may be different from what you're used to.

In a merger, each practice doesn't just reap the benefits of the other's clients and reputations—they also take on any advisors and employees who come with the practice. This can be a tricky proposition. I know of one advisor who merged his business with another firm. The advisor promised to integrate into and work within that practice's system. However, within a few months, he lost interest in working. He stopped recruiting clients, communicating with his peers, or adapting to the new system. This behavior not only hurt his clients but also communicated to his partners that they had made a mistake; they would never reap the benefits of either his clients or his cooperation.

In short, a merger is like a marriage—it must be founded on mutual trust, reliability, and respect. If you choose to merge with another firm, prepare to be flexible. Willingly integrate into their systems, accept their help, and treat them as your new team. The health of your clients and future depends on it.

Here's one thing to consider when selling your practice or joining another firm: Don't BS the other advisor! Be truthful. Don't say, "I always call my clients every quarter to check in" or "I have standardized portfolios for all of my clients" if you don't. You may strive to make those things happen, but if you're not there yet, don't exaggerate. If you exaggerate, the buyer will eventually find out, and it will cost them a lot of time and money to address.

"THE GLIDE PATH"

Somewhere between a succession plan and an internal or external sale lies what I like to call the glide path. In this scenario, you sell your book to another practice but continue managing your clients, slowly reducing your hours until a smooth transition has been completed. Some advisors choose to join another firm first, and then if it feels like a good match, sell their book to another advisor there. Others sell first and then move to the buyer's firm to work for a limited period—an approach I've found particularly effective. The seller sticks around for a certain period, earning a salary and continuing to serve their clients. This dramatically reduces attrition and keeps the payout high. You can also consider doing what we call a "flip-flop." This is where an advisor becomes an associate advisor, and an associate becomes the primary advisor. Whatever "tapered" approach you use allows you to reduce stress and responsibilities, and you glide into retirement.

KEY TAKEAWAY

Succession plans and the outright sale of your practice each have advantages. Succession plans move gradually, while selling to someone can be completed in a year. One enables you to continue working while the other offers a quick, clean break. You generally will be able to handpick and groom your successor over a longer period in a succession plan. You may have a shorter period to get to know your successor in an outright sale, but the competitive bidding process may result in a higher sales price. It all comes down to your needs and the needs of your business.

A third option—and sadly one of the most common—is to close your doors and quit working with no plan whatsoever. This kind of attrition doesn't help anyone—you, your client, and your fellow financial planners, who may be happy to take over your book and pay you for that opportunity. Don't let this happen to you! Although succession plans and practice sales may have been foreign concepts when you first started working as an advisor, today, it is a well-defined process. There are plenty of resources—starting with the book you hold in your hands right now—to help you. There are also experts in the field willing to guide you through the process.

Whether you choose a succession plan or decide to sell your practice, the key to avoiding a devastating fire sale is to plan. And the next step in making that plan is to determine just how much your business is worth. In the next chapter, we'll explore how to do that.

WHAT'S YOUR PRACTICE WORTH?

HERE'S A PRETTY TYPICAL CONVERSATION I OFTEN HAVE with other financial advisors:

PAUL: "So you ever think about transitioning out of the business?"

FINANCIAL ADVISOR: "Sure, I get calls from interested parties once in a while. But I just tell them I'm not ready or that I don't know."

PAUL: "Don't know if you're ready to get out of the business? Or are you saying you don't know what you stand to make?"

FINANCIAL ADVISOR (looking sheepish): "Well, both. What are practices even selling for?"

PAUL (going for casual): "Oh, you know… Somewhere in the range of two and a half times recurring revenue."

FINANCIAL ADVISOR: "Two and a half? Really?"

PAUL: "Yep. Sometimes more. Plus one times nonrecurring in many cases. If you prepare well for the sale, you might even hit three times recurring. And there have never been more buyers."

At this point in the discussion, their eyes widen, and they stare off into the distance as they begin their mental calculations. It can be hard for advisors to picture letting their meticulously crafted businesses go. But receiving double or triple their annual revenue all at once? That tends to get their attention.

If these sales figures surprise you, you're not alone. Most advisors aren't aware of what books are selling for and, therefore, what their own books might be worth. In my experience, this is simply because so many use the "lone wolf" model. They work in offices by themselves, with maybe a spouse acting as an assistant. They don't communicate with their peers or follow what's happening in their industry. Add this to the fact that a surprising number of advisors don't sell their book at all—they simply close their doors—and it's no surprise that sales values aren't more widely discussed.

So how can you start determining the value of your practice? Here are a few questions to consider as you move ahead.

SHOULD I GET A PROFESSIONAL VALUATION OF MY PRACTICE?

If you're within five years of retirement, it's wise to get a regular valuation of your practice. A valuation report will show you what your practice is likely worth and how it compares to other practices that are about the same size. A valuation can help you see if you met your annual goals for revenue growth or client type, or average client age. It can also point out where you should focus future efforts. If you're lagging behind comparable firms in your percentage of affluent clients, you might look into adding more or shedding some of your lower-wealth clients to improve your percentages. You might also see that your expenses are higher than your contemporaries and take steps to reduce your overhead. This depends on the size of your practice.

Let's make some distinctions here about the size of your practice. Consultant David Grau, in his book *Buying, Selling, and Valuing Financial Practices*, notes that independently owned financial planning practices fall into four categories:

1. **A job (or a book):** This is a typical "lone wolf" operation. A single person works for his clients. They don't have a formal office or paid employees and typically earn less than $200,000 a year. This category represents about 70 percent of the industry.

2. **A practice:** This is a small operation built around a practitioner. There might be some support staff, an office, computers, software, and a Customer Relationship Management (CRM) system. They usually operate as an S corporation or an LLC. This category represents about 25 percent of the industry. According to Grau, these operations often command a higher sales price and are easy to transition to a buyer.

3. **A business** has a more formal structure, and the revenue stream may be more diversified, although 75 percent typically comes from fees paid on managed accounts. These account for about 4 percent of the industry.

4. **A firm** is "an established, multi-owner, multigenerational business," and earnings primarily determine its success. About 90 percent of the revenue is fee based. These account for 1 percent of the industry, but this category is growing.

The valuation process for each category varies considerably, as does the cost.

If your book is small (it delivers gross revenue of less than $100,000 from the assets under management), then a professional valuation—which can cost upward of $1,000—is likely not worth the money. Remember that "2.5 times your annual revenue" figure I mentioned earlier? Under current market conditions, I'd consider that calculation a decent rule of thumb. If your book is on the leaner side, a third-party valuation will likely estimate low, resulting in you undershooting that 2.5x mark. Assuming your practice is small, I'd recommend skipping the valuation and presenting your 2.5x figure to potential buyers. (Keep in mind that any rule of thumb has its pitfalls. As the market changes, so will the typical sale price, forcing that rule-of-thumb calculation either up or down.)

On the other side of this coin, conducting a third-party valuation will certainly be advantageous if your book is more robust. Picture your sale like a real estate deal. One person wants to sell a house, and another wants to buy one. You can get a realtor if you wish to, or you can opt to make the deal between the two of you. But the more expensive the property, the more likely one or both parties will want to know its specific value to ensure they're getting a fair deal. Just as a real estate agent can compare the value of recent sales in a neighborhood—comparing the size, quality, and age of the homes in question—a professional valuator can compare your book with similarly sized sales. And this valuation gains credence in the eyes of potential buyers because it originates from a third party, not the seller.

Our firm recently purchased two small practices, and we didn't get a valuation for either. The price was so low that we didn't think it was necessary, and neither did the sellers. But if we were buying a larger, more complex practice, I would get a professional valuation before buying. If it's a large enough transaction to involve a bank, the lending institution will no doubt want a professional valuation of the practice. The firms that do these valuations recommend all advisors—even those not contemplating a sale—get valuations of their practice annually or at least biennially. An annual valuation helps measure your success for the year and helps you stay focused on following the best practices for maintaining or improving the quality of your practice.

In a sale, the buyer typically pays for the valuation. When we're pursuing an acquisition, I'll often order a valuation of the practice we're targeting and use the result to convince the seller to move ahead with the deal. Getting a valuation proves your commitment but also creates a sense of obligation on the seller's part. Moreover, the valuation number will be based on data from thousands of sales, lending it great credence. That alone might convince the seller to go through with the sale, particularly if the number is far higher than expected.

I also recommend conducting annual valuations starting several years before you intend to sell. Why? Because the best time to plant an apple tree is a decade before you need the fruit. Administering regular valuations will enable you to see when your tree could be mulched, fertilized, or pruned to improve its value over time. When it's time to sell, you want your business to be as healthy, prosperous, and appealing to buyers as possible.

HOW ARE PRACTICES TYPICALLY VALUED?

Whether your valuation is conducted internally or externally, the value of your book is usually based on a few factors: recurring revenue, product mix, client demographics, and client engagement.

RECURRING REVENUE

I was recently reading the listing for a practice put up for sale. Among other things, the ad bragged that the practice has $100 million in assets. An impressive figure, to say the least—and even more so when you consider that if their clients were paying the typical annual fee of 1–1.5 percent, this practice would be pulling down $1 million or more in annual revenue.

But it's not. As I dug further into the listing, I saw that this multimillion-dollar practice earns only about $250,000 annually. How does this happen? It's likely that this practice still conducts much of its business under the old model of selling financial products for an up-front commission rather than taking the revenue as an ongoing income stream. Although the rest of this practice's assets might have some intrinsic value, they're static, earning little or no ongoing revenue.

Many lone-wolf advisors work this way; they get addicted to the immediate bumps in commission income generated from selling their clients annuities or commission-based mutual fund rollovers from a brokerage account. But a managed account, in which the advisor's revenue increases as the account grows in value, pays more in the long run.

PRODUCT MIX

How diversified are the products you're offering to your clients? Do you sell annuities, mutual funds, certificates of deposit, money market accounts, and life insurance policies, for example? Depth of product offering shows a commitment to a comprehensive advice approach. The more products an individual client has, the deeper and stickier that client relationship is likely to be. The more assets and products you sell, the higher the value of your practice.

CLIENT DEMOGRAPHICS

To estimate your book's likely health and longevity, we also assess several key demographics of your client base. How old is your average client? If they're at or nearing retirement, this could mean that they've reached the peak of their wealth and are bringing you solid recurring revenues. Regrettably, however, it could also mean that they have fewer years left than younger clients, which translates to a shorter time as clients in your book.

Another key demographic is the average wealth you're managing for each client. Let's say that a practice has 400 clients but only 20 are "high value"—that is, only 100 have $1 million or more under management. The other 300 might have a $35,000 brokerage account and perhaps a small insurance policy. High numbers of lower-value clients will not be appealing to many buyers and not just because their recurring revenues will be small. In many, if not most, cases, it takes just as much time and effort to service a client with $10,000 as one with $10 million.

The ideal client has over $500,000 in assets, and an

ideal practice will have 80 percent or 90 percent of their clients with at least that much in their portfolios. In a perfect world, those with less should be the children of your wealthy clients because that shows your practice has some generational continuity, and you're not likely to lose all of Mom and Dad's money when they die. A book with 1,000 clients but with 850 portfolios of under $100,000 is far less appealing. You can't do a good job servicing that many people, and the fees from such small portfolios are not much of a convincing sales feature.

CLIENT ENGAGEMENT

We will also consider how actively you engage with your clients and vice versa. Do you run online marketing? Do you keep in regular contact via email campaigns? Can your clients use your website to interact directly with their accounts and advisors? If you want to see how committed clients are to your professional relationship, consider whether they use your online resources to keep a power of attorney or bank on file. Such clients are much more likely to stick with your practice through a transition, which is very appealing to buyers.

Are you engaging with your clients more directly, such as through client appreciation events, seminars, dinners, and fun events such as cooking or art classes? In a systematic way and not just the occasional one-off? Not everyone does this type of marketing, but if you're doing it regularly, it's a factor that will increase the value of your practice.

Overall, client satisfaction can also affect your book's value. A company can claim $100 million in assets all day long, but if a valuator discovers that your client satisfaction ratings are low—or worse, that clients are leaving your practice in droves—those assets won't mean much.

Many firms maintain a survey in their client portal, and evaluators will consider those results. Do your clients say you are providing valuable advice? Are you returning calls promptly? Do you put your clients' interests above your own?

Your buyer might also review your Customer Relationship Management system. First and foremost, do you have one? It's pretty remarkable how many advisors don't track client contact in any systematic way. And if you have a system, are you using it? How many client accounts have a note in them? Have notes been added to the client accounts in the last ninety days? Is other information noted in the Remarks section that shows a deeper level of client engagement? For example, there might be remarks like "Prefers to be called instead of emailed" or "Likes her coffee with cream."

A TALE OF TWO PRACTICES

Similar Assets, Vastly Different Values

Let's compare two practices that each have $100 million in assets but have starkly different approaches to managing their clients' investments. How do their sales values differ?

One practice put more emphasis on large, up-front commissions. Let's call this practice the Short-Term Cash Generator but Exit Value Slacker.

Thirty percent of this practice's business is in annuities, where the advisor earned his money in up-front commissions. The $30 million in annuities carry surrender charges for seven to ten years, so they can't easily be repositioned to a revenue-generating investment option. Essentially, the money is locked up. Another $20 million of this practice's business is tied up in real estate investment trusts (REITs) and business development companies (BDCs). Again, the advisor who put their clients' money into these investments earned a one-time up-front commission, but these funds typically have a holding period of seven to fifteen years. Twenty million dollars is in front-loaded mutual funds, where the advisor again took the up-front commission. These generate a 25 basis point trail, though, so it's not a total loss. The remaining $30 million is in managed accounts that earn the advisor about $300,000 annually in recurring revenue. With the mutual fund trail, the practice has about $350,000 in annual gross recurring revenue.

Now let's compare the Exit Value Slacker to the second practice, which eschewed the lure of up-front commissions in favor of longer-term investments. Let's call the second practice the Lean Mean Money Machine.

The Money Machine has 85 percent of its assets—$85 million—in managed accounts. It's invested in a diversified array of investment vehicles growing steadily. The advisor isn't earning any commissions but is taking a 1 percent annual wrap fee on that $85 million, earning about $850,000 a year. The remaining assets are longer-term investments, including accounts set up by the advisor's clients for their grandchildren. These offer small recurring revenue—perhaps a quarter of 1 percent—and the money is expected to stay in these accounts for another fifteen years.

The two practices differ in other ways. The average client age of the Exit Value Slacker is seventy-five, and the average client age for the Money Machine is sixty-one. The Exit Value Slacker has 450 clients, but the advisor hasn't contacted three-quarters of those clients since he initially sold them their annuities, REITs, or BDCs. The Money Machine has 100 clients, and the advisor regularly contacts them using a system he manages through his CRM software. He regularly schedules visits with them and proactively offers advice on retirement planning, insurance needs, estate topics, and tax strategies. Even their staffs are different. The Exit Value Slacker advisor's wife works for him part time. The Money Machine advisor has a veteran, licensed paraplanner who loves her job and has no plans to leave.

So what are each of these practices worth? The general starting point is that a practice is worth about 2.5 times its recurring revenue. But that rate can be affected by several factors, including the average age of clients and the quality of the advisor's office and operation. With that in mind, buyers interested in acquiring the Money Machine practice might be willing to pay three times recurring revenue. In addition, they would also want to pay one time the non-recurring revenue because they eventually will have an opportunity to manage that money and earn fees from it. The advisor has a skilled, professional staff person and a system for proactively reaching out and engaging with clients. The Cash Generator advisor, meanwhile, has a part-time family member who isn't likely to stay with the practice after he retires, and no outreach to speak of. His buyers can use that to reduce their multiplier down to 2.25. So let's do the quick math and multiply the recurring annual revenue by the multiplier:

Practice #1: Short-Term Cash Generator but Exit Value Slacker

$350,000 × 2.25 = $787,500

Total practice value: *$787,500*

Practice #2: A Lean Mean Money Machine

$850,000 × 3 = $2,550,000

$150,000 × 1 = $150,000

Total practice value: *$2,700,000*

So as you can see, although both practices have $100 million in assets under management, their respective values are hugely different. By foregoing the commissions to sell products that lock up a client's money for years, the Lean Mean Money Machine takes home 70 percent more revenue each year and is worth 140 percent more on the open market.

HOW ARE FORMAL APPRAISALS CONDUCTED?

In most formal valuations, third-party firms use proprietary formulas to gauge your practice's value. They look at the number of products you offer, the variety of those products, and your average revenue per client. Some firms will use a market-based approach that compares key metrics between your practice and other practices of a similar size. They will consider how much these other practices sold for to arrive at a price for your business.

Other consultants follow a mergers-and-acquisition approach that uses a "discounted earnings" method. Others use a combination of these to arrive at a value for your practice. Often, they provide a range your book will fall within because the actual value will also consider the terms of the sale, the financing structure, and assumptions made by the buyer and seller. All those factors can affect the final price.

Some valuations not only model your current practice value but predict how its value will change over time based on your client makeup. This considers your projected growth rate and helps you decide whether to sell now or wait.

In arriving at a valuation, these firms compare your profits to similarly sized firms, factoring in operating expenses to see how your financial efficiency compares to the industry benchmarks. They also consider how many advisors and staffers work in your office and compare their revenue and AUMs to similar firms. For each data point, you can see where you are on par, surpassing, or lagging behind the industry benchmarks.

Along the way, the evaluator will break down each data point. For example, when you look at affluent clients with over $500,000 in assets, how does your percentage compare to the industry standard? How does your average revenue per client compare? How does your clients' average age compare? Some firms even take a stab at measuring the goodwill of your firm's clients.

Part of most of these valuations is a section on recommended ways to improve your practice's value. This feature makes annual valuations a good idea for some financial planners. Each report takes into account factors that drive up a practice's value (recurring revenue, operating profit, percentage of high net worth clients) and factors that drive the value down (number of low-value clients, older clients, number of professionals on staff).*

There are two ways that practices are valued. The first is described above—using averages from other practice sales, taking into account factors listed, such as the client's age, and so forth. These standard valuations run about $1,300.

If it's a bigger practice—say over $2 million in GDC—you'll likely be asked to do a more robust valuation. This approach is similar to a traditional business valuation. The buyer will want to dig into your financials a little more deeply. You may have $2 million in gross revenue, but net revenue will

---

* Source: "Driving Practice Value," Advisor Legacy, Troy, Michigan.

be critical. This type of valuation may be around $5,000 or more.

You may be asking, "Paul, is it worth it to spend this kind of money for valuation? After all, I've been offered valuations for as little as $250. I get email offers for a 'valuation' for free as long as I give them my email address." Yes, it is worth it. Your low-cost or free valuation will consist of not much more than taking your recurring revenue and multiplying it by 2.5 times. You absolutely should spend the money and get a real valuation if you approach the sale of perhaps your largest asset in a way that maximizes your sale price.

A REAL-LIFE EXAMPLE

In 2020, my team hired a firm to value a practice we were thinking of buying. This firm used traditional merger-and-acquisition principles, market knowledge, and real-life case studies to arrive at a valuation. Their report went deeper than just numbers, taking into account the "nonprice" factors like staff, office size, quality, and other "soft" characteristics to arrive at a price range.

As expected, it broke down how much the seller made via recurring and transaction-based revenue. Its benchmark analysis compared the seller's gross revenue growth (GDC), percentage of recurring revenue, average client assets under management, average client age, the average length of the client relationship, and other metrics to the benchmark. Benchmarks are established from hundreds of practice valuations the firm has conducted in recent years.

The seller was lagging behind several benchmarks, including recurring revenue (71 percent vs. the benchmark of 88.5 percent), average client gross revenue ($1,372 vs. $3,284), average client AUM ($180,919 vs. $414,862), and average length client relationship (7 years vs. 15 years). Ninety percent of the seller's clients had less than $500,000 in their portfolio, and about half had less than $100,000. All of these levels were below the benchmark.

Where did they get these benchmarks? Many firms do so many valuations that they have great data on other practices that have come up for sale.

The valuation firm also analyzed the book's financial efficiency and found that our seller exceeded the operating profit benchmark. It brought home about $22,000 more revenue per year than the benchmark by keeping operating and overhead expenses low. It made less than the benchmark in revenue per client, but it spent about a third as much on client-related expenditures.

With all this data and perspective, the valuation showed that the fair market value for the practice was $460,000, or 2.77 times the book's recurring revenue. Not bad. But there was room for the advisor to boost his book's value. He needed fewer basic clients and more affluent ones. He needed to find some younger investors since his clients were slightly older than the benchmark age of sixty-one. He would also benefit from increasing the percentage of his income from recurring revenue from 70 percent to closer to 90 percent.

This advisor has yet to pull the trigger and sell. He's still working and hanging on because he doesn't know what else he could do to generate the kind of income he's making with so little work. We're hoping he'll decide to retire, though, because historically, he hasn't handled economic downturns well. And since he's only working twenty-five to thirty hours a week, he's not giving himself enough time to properly manage his clients' finances in a tricky economy. He either needs to return to full-time work or sell to someone willing to work full time for his clients.

WILL MY VALUATION REFLECT MY SALES PRICE?

The short answer is no. Valuation is a starting point and won't directly translate into your sales price. Think of it again like selling a house. Just because an appraiser or real estate agent determines that your home is worth half a million dollars, that doesn't mean the market will agree.

We recently bid on a practice where the seller used an outside firm to handle the sale. We received an offer sheet showing an asking price of $1.5 million. During our due diligence, we asked if a practice valuation had been completed, and if so, if we could see it. They were fine with providing it, and it showed a value of $1.2 million, or 20 percent less than the asking price. There were some other quirks with this practice. The seller was expecting the buyer to lease his office space for three years at significantly above the current market rates (with HOA fees of over $800 per month), keep his staff for a certain period, and a few other things that we considered unattractive. He was also an old-school brokerage guy, managing money but offering little else in the way of advice.

Guess where we bid? Right at the market valuation, knowing quite well that there probably was another sucker willing to go all-in. Sure enough, there was, and even though we didn't get this deal, we felt we dodged a bullet.

OFFER SHEETS

Two Examples of Practices for Sale

Here are two examples of offer sheets from advisors who are selling their practice. The first example is from an advisor's firm.

Immediate merge opportunity with succession in three to five years

- Seeking advisor to join team in mature investment management/advisory practice with long-standing presence in the Colorado market.
- Merge now, assist in enterprise growth, with succession in three to five years.
- Revenue is diverse with recurring revenues (trails and advisory fees) averaging 40 percent and commissions at 60 percent.
- Ideal candidate:
    - Five to ten years' experience
    - Series 7 and Series 65 or Series 66
    - Experience with retirement planning (both accumulation and distribution). Investment allocation, portfolio management, and advice are desirable.
- **AUM:** $96 million
- **Number of accounts:** 150–200 households
- **Revenue (three-year average):** $600,000

This next example is a more detailed offer sheet from an agent representing the seller.

The purpose of this outline is to define the intentions, terms, and structure of the opportunity for the buyer to purchase the practice of the seller. The outline should be understood as broadly defining "the intentions" of the two parties to facilitate a formal binding agreement completed by an attorney, which may substantially alter the language, but not the terms, below. Any tax considerations, explicit or implied, in this outline are for illustration purposes only; all tax-related advice should be provided by the tax professionals of the buyer and seller.

Sale Price

- $1,200,000
- Down payment (bank financed)
  - $1,020,000 (85 percent)
  - Due at closing
- Balance due (bank financed or buyer cash/escrow agent option)
  - $180,000 (15 percent)
  - Paid in full seven months after closing, adjusted per the attrition measurement.
  - A potential price reduction, resulting from the attrition measurement, is facilitated by but not limited to the balance due.
  - 5 percent interest (starts at closing)
  - Balance due terms and structure may be adjusted per the primary lender's requirements.
  - Bank financing in excess of the down payment amount can be held in escrow and released after the attrition measurement is made. Escrow services are typically paid for by the seller.

Attrition

Client assets will be measured at closing and compared to a second measurement to take place six months after the client transfer date. Client/asset attrition will be defined as a reduction in client assets resulting from clients leaving or passing away during the measurement period (not from stock market valuation or net flows). A 5 percent allowance will be given—up to 5 percent attrition will be allowed with no change in the purchase price. Attrition exceeding 5 percent will reduce the purchase price (by adjusting any remaining note) by subtracting

5 percent from the attrition amount (example: 7 percent attrition – 5 percent allowance = a 2 percent reduction in the purchase price).

- Clients voluntarily reassigned by the buyer will not be considered attrition.
- Client assets retained by another client in the practice will not be considered attrition.
- Clients who leave the practice but are compelled to leave certain assets behind (annuities, REITs, etc.) will be counted as attrition for the assets they remove.

Tax Allocation

- Goodwill: 98 percent (capital gains for seller; amortized over fifteen years for buyer)
- Consulting: 0 percent (ordinary income for seller; expense deduction for buyer); the seller will continue to work "in the practice" after the closing based on a separate compensated consulting agreement provided by the buyer.
- Fixtures: 0 percent
- Noncompete: 2 percent
  - The noncompete/nonsolicitation length and terms to be defined according to the requirements of the state the seller's practice resides in.
  - The tax allocation for your specific deal should result from a consultation with your tax professional.

Closing Date

- August 2022 (target date)
  - The specific date to be selected based on bank funding and client transition considerations.
  - Closing dates are often the day after the seller's compensation cutoff date.

Transition

- The seller will support the successful transition and ongoing service (of a select client group) for a period ending March 31, 2023.
  - The buyer will provide a separate consulting agreement to define the seller's compensation during the transition period.
  - Transition activity to be mutually agreed upon by the buyer and seller.
- Other terms (other terms define an understanding but may not be included in the asset purchase agreement):
  - All practice expenses will become that of the buyer after the closing date, including the seller's AMPF affiliation expenses to support the transition.
  - The buyer will assume the lease of the entire office space owned by the seller and sublease space to the existing tenants.
  - The buyer will retain the two existing support staff through the transition period, with the opportunity for ongoing employment, per the mutual agreement of the staff and buyer.
  - The due diligence period, limited to the terms defined above, will be considered to be completed with the acceptance of the above terms.

KEY TAKEAWAYS

Many factors will affect your practice valuation. Although most buyers will be concerned first and foremost with the hard numbers of recurring revenue, you must consider other factors to maximize your sales price. It's not uncommon for buyers to want to cherry-pick the best clients from your book and omit the rest, so prepare for that possibility.

At the start of this chapter, we discussed how uncommon it is for advisors to comprehend the true value of their books. Now that you're uncovering what you stand to make from your sale, the next logical question becomes, what would be the right sales terms for the sale of your book?

5

CHOOSING THE RIGHT PAYOUT

A FEW YEARS AGO, A FRIEND OF MINE—I'LL CALL HER LISA—decided she was ready to sell her book but not ready to quit working. So rather than a traditional lump-sum sale, Lisa brought her book to a larger firm in exchange for partial ownership of the bigger firm. Of course, taking ownership—like buying stock—can be a perilous form of payout. What if the firm falls on hard times or one of its partners runs into costly legal or regulatory troubles?

Most often, the risks stem from not carefully vetting the new firm. For example, we are trying to lure a local advisor to leave his firm and join our team, but he is cautious. When he joined his current firm five years ago, he was promised he would be one of the successors when the founding advisor retired. He was also promised staff support and a partnership role that would allow him to help make business decisions. None of that came to pass. The retiring advisor decided she wanted another female advisor to take over, and his plan to be one of her successors evaporated. Our candidate never developed a rapport with the other advisors in his new office or got the clerical help he expected. Now that he's considering a move to our firm, he's asking for everything in writing. Once bitten, twice shy! That was a smart move on his part.

Although there is always some risk, Lisa's move paid off big time for her. Whereas her own business had been increasing at a rate of 5–6 percent a year, the larger firm grew like gangbusters—upward of 30 percent. Lisa greatly contributed to the firm's growth because she now had the staff support that freed her to service clients and bring new clients to the firm. When she was ready to retire, her percentage of the business was worth far more than when she first joined the firm.

Just as there are myriad options for structuring your sale or succession, there are also many for your compensation. To choose the right one, you should consider various factors, including how large your business is, how long you intend to work, how quickly you'd like to be paid, and whom you envision at the wheel of your company in the future. Read on for some of the most common payout structures chosen by outgoing financial advisors like you.

WHAT PAYOUT STRUCTURES ARE OUT THERE?
OWNERSHIP PERCENTAGE

We've already seen how my friend Lisa benefited from moving her book to a larger firm in exchange for partial ownership of the business. In some deals, that compensation comes as stock but more often as a percentage in the company.

In that type of sale, you join another firm and get a certain amount of equity. In Lisa's case, her book was worth 15 percent of the overall business, so she became a 15 percent owner of that corporation. You'll also likely receive a salary and bonus for the few years you're working toward retirement, depending on your contract. The hope then becomes—as any financial advisor knows—that the new corporation's value will increase during those pre-retirement years, also increasing the value of your own "stock." When the time comes to retire, your partners buy you out, ideally leaving you with more money than your business would have made before the sale and partnership.

SELL AND STAY

Another option is to sell your book to a larger firm or another advisor within your existing firm and then choose to remain and work. The advantage here is twofold: you get the immediate benefit of the large payout, but you also get to keep enjoying your working schedule and environment and the comfort of a continuous income stream. The new firm benefits by having you help maintain the client relationships and having your years of experience.

But some advisors struggle in their new roles. They may have to step down a notch, and simply serving clients may seem mundane compared to being the big cheese. Often, they join an office with very different practices than they are used to, and it's hard to remain quiet when your instincts are shouting, "Hey, that's my client! We do things differently!" It can be emotional, so think long and hard before you settle on this option. We once bought a practice from an older advisor and offered him a part-time job servicing clients. He helpfully transitioned his clients to us but did little beyond that. His skills were outdated, and to us, he seemed like he was moving in slow motion. Nevertheless, he wanted to teach us complex options strategies or esoteric brokerage trading platform tricks we would never use. We needed someone to quickly and efficiently take care of clients, and he didn't have that ability. His part-time employment ended within six weeks.

A JUNIOR PARTNER BUYING IN TRANCHES

If you've read Chapter 2, this model will sound familiar—a succession plan in which you pass your business over to a younger partner at your firm over time. As we've established, there are numerous professional benefits here, including a minimum disruption to clients, since your successor will be working off the same system as you and will have ample time to get to know your clients' unique needs before you depart.

But how does this model usually function from a payout standpoint? Let's say that your successor plans to buy up tranches of your book over the next three years, at which point they will become the full owner. You will want to ensure that you have an agreement stipulating how compensation will be handled during this period of shifting ownership. Will your successor be compensated for any clients currently under their purview? Paid extra as they onboard new clients?

As mentioned previously, experienced advisors must realize that young people can be flaky sometimes. Younger generations change jobs and careers far more than baby boomers ever did, so you must be prepared if your chosen successor suddenly decides to take his talents to a new profession. It happens all the time. You also must be prepared to train and work with them to improve their skills. That takes time and preparation, and you must take this responsibility seriously. If your skillset is stagnant and you're a bit of a fuddy-duddy (let's face it, you think you're pretty cool, but the younger generation probably doesn't see you that way), your successor may lose faith in the arrangement. Find someone who can give the cutting-edge training a young advisor expects and needs. You might learn a thing or two yourself! Be honest—do you have the skills and desire to train someone?

Think, too, about your clients. If they are all as old as you are, how will they take to a fresh-faced youngster? When looking for a successor, look for someone you know your clients will trust and respect. I think the answer is finding a "youngish" partner—someone in their late thirties or early forties with some experience. Those individuals are hard to find, however—they're usually entrenched in their opportunities by that stage. But if you keep at it and look hard enough, you'll find the right person.

CLOSED SALE

As mentioned in Chapter 3, a closed sale occurs when a buyer and seller find each other and arrange a deal outside the open market. The terms of such a sale are determined by negotiation, but if a bank finances the sale, the seller will generally get paid out at closing. Little or no portion of the sale is carried by the seller.

FAMILY SUCCESSION

Many advisors see the appeal of selling their books to successors within their own families. Who wouldn't want to ensure that their meticulously crafted practices benefit those they care for most? Unfortunately, family-succession plans can be fraught with tension.

In most cases, expecting your son or daughter to take over your business is a mistake! You're likely taking the easy way out—picking what may be the only young person you know. Let's be honest: in most cases, your kid doesn't deserve this opportunity, isn't qualified for it, and you may be trying to fit a square peg into a round hole.

For one thing, it's often the seller—the business builder—who's most interested in involving a family member. If you're considering this type of succession, ask yourself this: Are you certain that your son, daughter, spouse, or other family member is as dedicated to this field of business as you are? An advisor friend recently told me, "Oh, don't worry about my retirement. My wife is twelve years younger than me, so she will get licensed and take over my business when I go. Don't worry. I've got a plan." I'd love to hear the wife's perspective on this plan. Is she sure she wants to learn a new career at age fifty-five while her husband's hitting golf balls at the club?

My point is, don't assume that just because your family members love you, they'll automatically love to take over your book. Any half-hearted employee can quickly become a drain on your time and resources, especially when that employee is related to you. Many advisors begin grooming their children as successors, only to find that training a son or daughter is much different from training your average college graduate. Consider the experience from their perspective. If a boss says, "Make sure you close up these files by the end of the day this time," that will probably just feel like good, ordinary management. But if a parent says the same thing, it can feel like micromanagement or worse, a lack of trust. Add to this the fact that young folks are often flaky and unreliable, and you have a recipe for familial tension that could end in professional (and perhaps personal) disaster.

My son expressed interest in joining the financial advisory field. His interest is self-driven, but we decided he should gain experience at a big investment company like Charles Schwab or T. Rowe Price. After five or ten years, he'll have the option of joining me at my company—but only if he has developed the skills and mindset to be a great addition to our team. No special favors for him! I will not be the decision maker on whether he gets a chance with us, nor will I be his day-to-day manager.

LIFESTYLE SALE

You might also be interested in what I refer to as a lifestyle sale—a sale that grants you a particular schedule or degree of freedom in your personal life. Perhaps your ideal retirement would resemble the "tapered landing" discussed in Chapter 2. You'd join a larger firm, sell your book to another advisor, and then continue working but with a caveat as part of your contract. The buyer must make concessions to support your desired lifestyle, such as allowing you to work only part time or six months of the year.

The appeal here is obvious. Many advisors would love the security of a recurring paycheck and the freedom to lie on a beach in Florida or go snowmobiling in Montana when winter comes.

Regardless of any agreement at the time of sale, you may see a lot of tension and pushback from peers if your lifestyle makes you an unreliable, unpredictable coworker. Frequently, it's the buyer who must pick up your slack when you take off for another adventure, which may become a frustrating situation if you and your partners don't use the same systems or serve the same clients.

A lifestyle sale can throw such a wrench into buyers' working lives that many don't consider them worth the investment. So remember that even if you see the appeal of a lifestyle sale, potential buyers might not, which could limit your buyer pool.

HOW IS CLIENT ATTRITION HANDLED?

An attrition clause is almost always included in any sales contract to protect both a seller and buyer. Essentially, an attrition clause names which entity—buyer or seller—is responsible for clients who leave the new corporation by a certain date.

Attrition clauses can be tricky, so be sure to run yours by an attorney. For example, say your buyer has included a clause that states that they don't have to pay for any clients who leave within three months for any reason. Under this setup, nothing prevents the buyer from simply handing off any unwanted clients to another advisor within that three months. Usually, it's much longer than three months—more like one to two years—and you, as the seller, would receive no compensation for those clients.

On the flip side of that coin, buyers also have reason to be cautious. If the book they're buying is filled with dissatisfied clients, they could face a mass exodus within a month of acquisition. A strong attrition clause would protect these sellers from losing half the value of their new books.

WHAT ROLE DO BANKS PLAY IN SALES?

Banks are increasingly willing to loan money to advisors purchasing financial advising practices. For instance, Live Oak, a digital cloud-based bank operating in all fifty states, has focused on these recently. But most banks are still inexperienced in these transactions. That may change; some buyers using banks prefer conventional loans over Small Business Administration loans because the SBA requires so much paperwork.

Most banks will require the buyer to put down 10 percent or more and repay the loan over time. A typical loan period is ten years. That makes sense for many buyers who want to make sure they maintain their positive cash flow over time. Some sellers prefer a bank deal because it ensures they get their full payment at closing and not over an extended period.

WHEN THE SELLER CARRIES THE LOAN

Seller financing is quite common. Most sellers will carry the loan in return for regular payments over time. Seller financing simplifies getting to yes in your deal with the buyer. There may be compelling tax reasons to stretch your payments from the buyer over time rather than take a lump sum all at once. You may know the buyer well and have a high degree of trust.

There is risk, however. You will need clauses in your agreement with the buyer to protect you. For example, who will take over for the buyer and continue making payments to you if the seller dies or becomes disabled? What if the buyer declares bankruptcy?

COMPANY FINANCING

If you work for a large firm, the company may help finance an internal practice sale. They'll also offer favorable terms and may make a portion of the loan forgivable after several years. This makes borrowing easier but also ties you to the firm. We are also seeing more of the larger broker-dealers offer financing to their advisors when making external practice acquisitions. Applying for these loans is almost certainly easier than using an outside lender. If your buyer is using financing from their broker-dealer, it should give you a higher degree of confidence that the financing is actually going to be approved and your sale is going to happen in a timely fashion.

HOW DOES YOUR SALE AFFECT YOUR EMPLOYEES?

Depending on your situation and goals, selling your book might also mean transferring your employees to the umbrella of the new owner. This can be a considerable boon all around. On the buyer side, acquiring experienced employees means getting informed, astute insights into each new client, which can smooth and shorten transition times. On the employee side, joining a new corporation can mean better benefits and pay since the buyer is almost always a larger entity with greater means.

Unfortunately, some employees also find the changes inherent in a sale challenging or uncomfortable. For example, if your assistant has spent thirty years learning every quirk of your particular system, they might not be interested in learning a new one from scratch. It can be just as challenging—if not more so—for advisors. In one situation, a practice's employee became licensed to take over the business, but the lead advisor ultimately chose not to sell to her. Naturally, the employee resisted the sale and resented the new owners, creating unforeseen tension among the staff members and decreasing her value in the eyes of the company. The buyer had no idea that this dynamic existed until after closing the sale.

You care about your employees, so I recommend being as open with them as possible. As far as you're able, let them know what to expect regarding their changing leadership, duties, and benefits. Very few things are more destructive to morale than unrealistic, unmet expectations, so do your best to set them up for success.

You may have an employee you know will not be a good fit with the new team, yet you feel great loyalty to this person. Don't let your loyalty get in the way here. Be honest with the new team and the employee, and don't let that employee make the transition. You'll save yourself and your new team a lot of headaches and bad will.

KEY TAKEAWAY

You can monetize your practice in many different ways, so the path you choose will depend on your personal needs and circumstances. Are you ready to cut and run, or would you prefer to groom your successor? Do you want to continue working? How long do you want to invest in ensuring the new buyer is right for your clients? All these factors will affect your payout structure, so don't try and rush this choice.

My friend Lisa took the time to find the ideal solution for her situation: the opportunity to sell at the peak of her practice, seamlessly transition her clients to new advisors, and make a pile of cash to boot. However, not all sellers get so lucky. In our next chapter, we'll look at some real-life case studies of advisory sales—the good, the bad, and the ugly.

6

CASE STUDIES

EVERY SALE DIFFERS BECAUSE EVERY FINANCIAL PLANNER has different clients, employees, offices, and practices. Every advisor is different.

To give you a better sense of the selling process, I've pulled together a series of case studies that explain some of the challenges you might face in selling your practice or buying another advisor's book.

WHEN A SUCCESSION AGREEMENT BECOMES A FIRE SALE

Several years ago, I signed a succession agreement with Omar and his associate advisor, Biff, to buy their practices in the event of their death or disability.

A few months later, I got an email from Omar saying that he'd fired Biff. Biff, he said, had been harassing one of Omar's assistants. It wasn't sexual harassment but stemmed from Biff's belief that the assistant was incompetent (which she was, but that's another story). After a particularly egregious error, Biff erupted and yelled at the assistant. Forced to intervene, Omar chose to keep his assistant and give Biff the heave-ho.

Within an hour after I saw the email from Omar, Biff was calling me. Biff told me about the split and said that, as a result, he was not only leaving the firm but retiring from the profession.

"Do you still want to buy my practice?" he asked.

Over the next few days, I learned that Omar had complete control over Biff's clients—even though Biff had joined Omar's practice with a pretty sizable book of his own—and was not interested in helping his former associate sell to me. When Biff and Omar became partners, they agreed that Omar would be the lead partner in the eyes of the broker-dealer. When they were getting along, this was a minor detail. But in an antagonistic split like this one, it's a very big deal. It gave Omar significant leverage in how Biff's book was managed.

For example, Biff and Omar's practice deducted their 1 percent advisory charge from their clients every quarter. This is typically a significant amount of money. But Omar, using his power as the franchise partner, delayed the book sale for two quarters so that he and not Biff could collect all of this revenue. Omar was playing hardball. He was out for blood.

It got worse. Omar immediately began contacting Biff's clients to retain them for himself. His letter to Biff's clients suggested that Biff had been let go for some unstated, nefarious reason. By the time Omar finished, Biff's $50 million book was down to $42 million in assets under management. Biff did all he could to reach out to his clients to reassure them, but over time, clients alarmed by the tone of Omar's letter continued to leave the firm, bringing Biff's assets under management down to $34 million. Biff's proceeds were based on that much-lower asset level. It was a tough outcome, but if Biff and I didn't have our succession plan in place, the result could have been much worse; Biff's entire book would have fallen under Omar's management. Biff would have had to negotiate directly with Omar on the sales price instead of having me help out as a semi-neutral third party.

WHEN THE SELLER RENEGED ON A DEAL

A few years ago, I set up a succession deal with a financial advisor we'll call Edward. I was to buy his practice in case of his death or disability.

In 2022, I learned Edward was retiring. Edward didn't inform me, however; I learned about it from a consultant helping Edward sell his practice. You'd think that since Edward had a succession agreement with me, he would have reached out personally, but that's not what happened. The consultant informed me that Edward was selling his practice, and he quoted a price 20 percent more than the appraised value of the practice. Would I like to make an offer?

I was skeptical. The consultant's price was based on the book's value three months earlier. Since then, the stock market had fallen about 20 percent, making the book worth much less. In my mind, their price was about 40 percent higher than the book's value in the current market. The deal also required we pay Edward a consulting fee *and* take over the lease on his offices, which he rented for almost twice the rate for comparable offices right around the corner.

Was I interested? Well, not really.

Nevertheless, I took the offer to my team members and asked what they thought. Should we buy it? Their response was swift and in line with my thinking: Not at that price! Meanwhile, the consultant got another firm interested in Edward's practice, hoping to start a bidding war. Their tactic didn't work.

Eventually, we submitted a bid, but it was much lower than the asking price. We didn't get the practice, and you know what? We weren't disappointed in the least.

I learned some valuable lessons. I do succession agreements differently now. In addition to death and disability, I include retirement and a right of first refusal in these agreements.

THE GREEN ASSOCIATE PLAN

I meet with my good friend John every three months or so. John, who is fifty-nine, is a successful financial advisor who works almost exclusively with doctors. He has an efficient practice of about $100 million, 100 clients, and almost all of it in a recurring revenue position.

Sadly, John has an incurable health condition. Every time we meet, he seems a little worse. He has increasing difficulty walking, and it's getting harder for him to talk. The disease will eventually force him out of business.

We've talked about setting up a succession plan so I can buy John's book when he decides he can no longer work. He would have to join my firm, but that won't work for him because he uses a different clearing firm and would be forced to file a mountain of paperwork. Unfortunately, that approach won't work for John. He would have to switch broker-dealers, and a significant part of his business isn't transferable to most other firms. Besides, he likes his broker-dealer, particularly their statements and reporting. He's also getting a generous consulting fee for his work on a big retirement plan for a local educational institution, and that $60,000-a-year payment wouldn't transfer. His best option would be to transfer to a new firm with a simple transfer process and the same clearing firm. That way, he's not forced to "repaper" all his clients.

Still, he needs to do *something*. Unfortunately, his latest plan isn't a very good option either.

Instead of joining another practice and following a well-marked path to succession, John plans to bring on a green associate to help run his office and take over his book when he retires. When I say "green," I'm not joking. The associate he picked out is still in college. He's still a year and a half from graduating. John met him online and began a dialogue about moving to Colorado and joining John's practice.

"You hired him without meeting him first?" I asked over lunch one day.

"Well, I got to know him online," John replied. "He's a real self-starter!"

"Has he ever been to Colorado?"

"No."

"Who is going to train him?"

"I will."

"Have you ever trained an advisor before?"

"No, but I'll share my knowledge, and he'll just have to jump in and learn! He understands that he'll have to learn and work mostly independently."

As you can tell from this exchange, I didn't think much of John's succession plan. I hired and trained *a lot* of young financial planners earlier in my career, and I found that it's not an easy process. They have a lot to learn. They have to learn how to absorb the pain of rejection when potential clients turn them down. They have to reassure clients even when they aren't sure themselves. They don't make much money.

As a manager, I would hire young people convinced financial advising was their dream job. It was all they ever wanted to do. Within a year, they were gone, often leaving financial advising to go into a completely unrelated field. One became a minister. One sold cars. Another became a tour guide. (All true!)

"I thought this was your dream job," I'd say, reading their resignation letters after I'd committed weeks and months to their training.

"Oh, it was," they replied. "But now I see that serving the Lord is my true calling."

I don't mean to denigrate all recent college grads or younger advisor candidates, but many are flaky. I hired one recent college graduate who had been recommended to me personally by the president of my alma mater. He was bright and energetic and keenly interested in financial planning. But he would make dumb mistakes, like the time he left our ground-floor office windows open all week-end with all our financial records and office equipment on full display and readily available for passing thieves. We didn't lose anything that time, but we eventually lost our young employee when his roommate recruited him to answer phones at the T. Rowe Price call center a few months later.

In John's situation, the future does not look very bright either. What are all those doctors going to think when John retires and suddenly their finances are managed by an inexperienced twenty-five-year-old? What happens on that day when John isn't in the office, and a client calls and says he's closing on a new house and selling his old one, and he needs help coming up with the money to bridge the difference? Should he pull from his portfolio, borrow it, or combine the two? The kid isn't going to have a clue.

As of this writing, John is still waiting for the protégé's arrival. I continue to have lunch with him every few months, and my goal is to get him to bring his book and his young colleague over to our firm so we can help with the transition after John retires.

A POOR CULTURAL FIT

When you're considering selling your practice or acquiring one, it's essential to determine if you are a good cultural fit with the other party. Do you both adhere to the same investing practices? Do you share the same client service philosophy? Are both sides open to learning from the success of your new partners?

Part of my reason for emphasizing this is because of the experience we had acquiring the practice of an advisor in our town who managed a small practice. That deal was full of surprises. Once the deal was made and the transition started, both sides greeted the other with similar uncomprehending, quizzical looks. *You do it* that *way? Why?* Let me explain.

I met Mike after seeing that his practice was up for sale on one of the buying and selling websites I subscribe to. Usually, there are sixty or so buyers for each seller on these sites, so it's not the best way to meet advisors who are thinking of selling. But this practice was in my city, which surprised me because I didn't recognize the seller's name. But I immediately reached out to the advisor, and we arranged to meet two days later.

Mike and I hit it off reasonably well, and he admitted that no one seemed eager to buy his book. His 500 clients were spread across many of the small towns in southern Colorado, and he had only about $17 million in assets under management. Most of his clients were friends and former colleagues, and none were particularly wealthy. Moreover, everyone—whether they had a $25,000 or a $250,000 portfolio—was invested the same way: an annuity, a small life insurance policy, and one or two mutual funds. Mike worked out of his house and stored all his files on paper in giant file cabinets. Almost no computer use. No website.

And very little advice from Mike. I visited with him several times and was there when clients called in. Each time, Mike gave the same advice: "It's fine. Just keep holding it."

I could quickly see why so few advisors had expressed interest in his practice. He had no service model—if he needed something, he just showed up at clients' houses unannounced. When I asked his clients about the last time they'd met with Mike, many gave me a quizzical look. "I haven't met with him since he sold me this stuff," they'd say. They trusted Mike, but they were mostly unsophisticated investors who didn't take kindly to an advisor from the city who wanted to talk about changing to a more suitable approach.

It got worse. Mike hadn't written down his clients' life insurance products' names, and most turned out to be an off-the-shelf product that wasn't transferrable. He was contemptuous of our computer systems, appointment scheduling, and investment recommendations. In retrospect, he would have been better off selling his book to an old-school advisor in some other small town.

Despite this, the transition went well. But Mike went into retirement feeling he sold his practice to the wrong team. We never developed a kinship with him. We don't even know where he is today.

BRINGING ON A SUCCESSOR WHO DOESN'T HAVE THE HUNGER FOR IT

My friend Jon is seventy-two years old and a successful advisor. He's been in the business for thirty-five years and is active in the community. Not long after the COVID-19 pandemic, I ran into him at a nice restaurant, and we chatted about our industry.

"Business is good, but I want to scale back," Jon told me.

"Do you have a successor?" I asked.

"No," he admitted. "I'm seventy-two, and I haven't figured out my exit strategy yet!"

I nodded and suppressed a smile. This was music to my ears. "We should talk," I said, and we made plans to have lunch next week.

We met at a local brewery, and he told me about his practice. His office is in a desirable downtown location. His longtime assistant runs the show, and his associate advisor helps him manage the accounts.

I asked about the associate. What's his role? Is he out hunting for new business, or is he providing service for Jon's low-dollar clients? Or does he handle the backstage administrative chores?

Jon shrugged. He hired the associate, Parker, to prospect for new clients—to network and pick up the phone and find new clients for the firm. Only it hadn't turned out that way. Parker could provide service to clients, but he lacked the hunger to recruit new business for the firm.

"Is he interested in buying the practice from you?" I asked. "Maybe he'd be more motivated to work if he knew $100 million in assets would become his to manage in just a few years."

Jon smiled.

"He doesn't need the money," he said.

It turns out that Parker was already independently wealthy. He'd inherited a fortune and didn't need to work it all. He enjoyed servicing clients but was not interested in running the office and managing employees. For him, the job was just a way to take a break from the golf course and keep an eye on the stock market.

So this is why Jon is still working, I thought. He hired a decent employee but a terrible candidate to be his successor.

I am talking to Jon about purchasing his book, but I understand that may not happen. At seventy-two, Jon may not want to transition his clients to a new firm. But we'll still work with him on his exit strategy. I believe we should always help fellow advisors with their transitions, even when we're not acquiring the business. I've introduced Jon to a skilled associate advisor who would love to take over the business, and we'll do what we can to help that exit strategy work for them. Parker, meanwhile, continues to work for the practice. He'll probably get a group of clients when Jon retires, or he may just continue working for the new firm.

A SUCCESSFUL COURTSHIP WITH AN ALIGNMENT OF VALUES AND GOALS

Richard is a fifty-five-year-old advisor with a national broker-dealer. He joined that firm several years ago with the promise that he would have staff and colleague support and a chance to succeed the senior partner when she retired. It was a handshake deal with nothing in writing.

The promises weren't kept. The firm's archaic systems made work tedious and slow. If Richard wanted to add a bank account to a client's accounts, the client had to sign a separate form for each account. When the senior partner approached retirement, she told Richard she'd made other succession plans and that he would not be able to buy the practice.

Once bitten, twice shy.

We approached Richard about joining our team. By joining us, we said, you can focus on what you love—meeting with clients and talking to prospects. We had staff who could do some of Richard's paperwork, handle his trades, and manage portfolios. Richard was eager to build his practice value and maximize his payout when he retires in five years, and we felt our team could help him achieve that.

We courted Richard for two years. During that time, we shared our team's core values and took the time to see if Richard shared those values. In turn, Richard saw how we embodied our core values in our daily work.

We insist that new team members share at least three of our five values. Otherwise, a partnership is likely to fail. By inviting Richard to team potluck dinners, lunch, and phone calls, we could see that he aligned with us.

At the same time, we needed to show Richard that we knew how to grow. We don't just talk about it. Our goal is to reach $10 billion in assets by 2031, and Richard wanted to know the steps, details, and timeline for that process. Richard's a former engineer, but I didn't hold that against him. He pushed us to improve our plans.

More importantly, we didn't make broad verbal assurances to Richard. Instead, we laid out a specific plan for pay, transition, and criteria for partnership. We explained the formula we used to calculate his equity. We detailed how many fee-based financial plans we expected him to complete. Richard's attorney and our attorney vetted everything. We didn't rush anything.

Richard joined us, and the transition wasn't always perfectly smooth. There were technological hiccups. But we had built trust and vision, so even when Richard got frustrated, we never lost our mutual respect and ability to move forward with our eyes on the big picture.

A VERY NICE MAN WHO CLEARLY NEEDED TO RETIRE

Charles was one of my first practice acquisitions. I met him at a training event in Colorado Springs. It was pretty clear he was a lone-wolf advisor and was under the radar of other potential buyers. He was sixty-eight when I met him, and he had a small book. He had switched firms three times over the years—most, it seemed, for the signing bonuses.

I met with him at his two-room office in a run-down building next to the railroad tracks. He had no managed accounts and little recurring revenue. He took up-front commissions on his mutual fund and annuity sales. Although he had about $15 million in assets, he was generating only about $50,000 annually in gross revenue.

He recognized that he should retire but had no idea what

he would do with himself. He appreciated having a place to go to every morning, and he usually brought his dog to the office.

At first, I made appointments to see him but soon learned that wasn't necessary. He was in the office every morning and usually went home by 1:00 p.m. I knew that if I dropped in by mid-morning, he would be at his desk.

Working? No. Watching Denver Broncos clips on YouTube? Listening to talk radio? Yes. Occasionally, the phone would ring, and a client would request a stock purchase or a money movement. Sometimes a client would drop by to say hello and visit but usually not to conduct business.

And what an office it was. The furniture was old and dated. His framed awards and family photos were ten or fifteen years old. The carpet was dirty, and he had a pile of files on his desk—no doubt left there unsecured when he went home, available to the nighttime office cleaners. The fifty-five-gallon fish tank was half-empty, covered in algae, and home to one angel fish and one carp. One day I saw a cockroach go strolling across his floor—shocking since I didn't know Colorado had such big cockroaches. All I could think was, "What must his clients feel like coming in here?"

Once a client dropped by to ask about a 529 plan for his son. Charles's advice to him was so profoundly wrong that I jumped in and corrected him. I hated to do that, but I couldn't let the client leave with such bad information.

Charles had reached a point where he needed to retire. He had a 1970s small-town stock broker skillset. His knowledge was outdated. His clients liked him, but he was doing nothing to serve them. His office was a wreck.

What's worse is that he didn't have any intention of retiring. I visited every month for two years, and it wasn't until his landlord increased his rent by about $300 per month that he finally agreed to sell. I bought his book for about $70,000. If he had 80 percent of his $15 million in assets as recurring revenue, his practice would have been worth $300,000. He wanted to be paid up front, but no bank was willing to finance a sale this small. He carried the note, and I paid him off over two years.

EVERYTHING GOES AS PLANNED

Ed is a veteran of the financial services industry. He's done it all—recruiting, training, managing, and advising investors as a senior leader in a local bank branch.

We courted him for years. We wanted him to work at our firm so we could set up a succession plan to acquire his practice when he retires in a few years. At first, Ed was open to the idea. He didn't feel his current firm's systems, processes, and service level was good enough for his clients.

The more I talked with Ed, the more apparent his motivations became. Money is not Ed's primary focus in transitioning out of the business. His main goal is to ensure his clients are happy. He's going to see these people in the community for years, and their success and his reputation are paramount to him.

Ed initially chose not to join us and make us his successors. His firm had recruited an internal successor and put a financial transition package together for Ed. Ed would work for two more years. In year one, he would introduce his clients to the new advisor, begin to transition the clients to her, and get paid the revenue generated. In year two, he would begin to transition out, work much less, and get paid less.

Upon retirement, he would receive a payout over the next five years from the firm. By year three, he would be retired.

When he told us he was going with this plan, he said, "It's not as much money as you offered, and there won't be a great team to support me as you have. But the advisor taking over is very sharp, and I think she'll do a good job with the clients. The best thing for me is that I don't need to go through the headache of transitioning my clients to a new firm at this point in my life."

We continued to stay in touch with him, and about six months later, we went to lunch with him. He wasn't happy. The succeeding advisor was fine, but his broker-dealer was as dysfunctional as ever. They were changing the terms of his succession and wanted him to sign a new agreement. He wasn't getting sufficient staff support. The broker-dealer didn't service Ed's clients well.

Ed had decided to delay his retirement by three years but wanted to reduce his workload. To do that, he felt he needed a more robust team around him. We could help him achieve a true glide path. His current broker-dealer would only allow full retirement.

Ed joined us in the fall of 2022. Over the next three months, 95 percent of his client assets were transferred with him. He is happy seeing his best clients, working part time, and spending the winter at his second home in Arizona. What made Ed's transition a success?

- He had already handed off about 100 clients with whom he didn't have strong relationships. He only transitioned 100 of his best relationships—the people who love him.
- He had a clear vision of what he wanted. He wanted the

freedom to take time off without worrying if his clients were getting outstanding service.

- He based his decision on his core values—taking care of his clients and finding meaning in continuing to work and serve others. He didn't base his decision on money alone.
- He followed our transition process. He didn't let his ego get in the way by second-guessing our practices or thinking he knew better "what's best for my clients." We've transitioned advisors many times and know what works. Most advisors transition once or twice and often don't know what's best.
- He approached the transition to the new firm thoughtfully and methodically. He identified potential problems and took action to resolve them. He would say, "I know this is going to be hard work, and I don't want to make it any harder than it needs to be because I didn't plan."
- His experience made him resilient. Even well-planned transitions are rarely problem-free, and Ed's emotional competence allowed him to roll with the punches.

As I noted at the beginning of this chapter, every sale or succession plan is different. The case studies I've presented here represent common pitfalls and illustrate how to create a great succession experience. In the next chapter, I'll describe the nuts and bolts of properly selling your practice or transitioning your book to another firm.

7

MAKING THE DEAL

IN SOME WAYS, SELLING YOUR PRACTICE IS LIKE SELLING any property or business. The big difference is that you're also selling the trust and relationships you've built with clients over the years. This can be a tricky proposition, emotionally speaking, because you're capitalizing on the goodwill you've established throughout your career. As a result, many sellers are more concerned with *whom* they are selling to than how much that buyer is paying them. They want their clients taken care of.

This concern was particularly apparent when my team and I became potential buyers for a large practice in Texas. The seller hired an outside firm to market the practice, and the firm did an excellent job. They helped the advisor get the book ready for sale. They even created a little video about the firm. Prospective buyers had to sign up through a website and provide details about their firm to be approved as qualified buyers. Those who made the cut were invited to a video call where prospective buyers could meet the seller and ask questions about the practice. On that call, the seller outlined what they were looking for in a buyer. Later, the marketing firm wanted details about our approaches to client engagement. We also had to submit our purchase offers.

In time, the field was whittled down to seven potential buyers. We were one of them. The seller's representative and the seller came back and interviewed us again. How often would we be coming to Texas to meet with clients? Would we have an office down there? Could we offer more than our original offer?

Our initial bid was as high as we could comfortably go and not as high as the $7 million the seller wanted for the client. We declined to go higher, but the seller eventually got both the money and the assurances that the buyers would maintain the book's integrity and was set up to service clients at the level the sellers wanted.

This is a great example of how to go about selling your book. With the help of an outside firm, the seller carefully vetted the interested buyers and took the time to get to know those buyers before making the deal. They got the price they wanted.

This is not to say you need a seller's agent. You may not want to pay that commission. But the story does reveal how important it is to get to know your buyer. Take the time to do this. There is a courting sequence in these deals, and the time you spend getting to know each other can reveal problems or provide valuable reassurances. This is one reason I spend so much time networking. I get to know prospective partners or sellers. I learn about their families, how they started their businesses, and their philosophy about serving clients.

We spoke recently with a seventy-three-year-old female advisor from Denver. She was interested in selling her practice, but she wasn't interested in the price. She loves her clients and wants someone who will take care of them. She has clients she doesn't make any money from, but she still takes them out to lunch. How often do you run into that? A lot of advisors will say they care about their clients, but not everyone means it. This lady did. This is how she paid back her clients' trust. She eventually sold her book to another advisor, but the time I spent getting to know her felt worthwhile.

WHAT PROFESSIONAL HELP SHOULD YOU HIRE TO AID THE SALE?

BROKER OR SALES AGENT

It's easy to argue against hiring a pro to represent your sale. After all, an agent will take a percentage of your proceeds, and there's no additional training required to broker a deal in our field, despite many pitfalls inherent to the process.

But I'd still recommend that you consider it.

Here's the thing about selling your practice. In all probability, the buyers making offers on your book—especially if you list on the open market—will have conducted several such deals before. However, this will likely be the only sale you ever make. That means there's a huge disparity in knowledge and experience, which can make negotiations a bit one-sided.

An experienced agent can help you spot deficiencies in your practice and ready your book for sale. They can also help with marketing and negotiations, taking the pressure off you to learn every angle of this process. Most of all, they'll do their best to ensure you get the best price possible since that also bolsters their bottom line. In my experience, hiring an agent tends to be a solid financial investment.

This isn't to say that any agent will do. Again, no additional licensing is required to sell a financial advisory practice, so you should be careful to choose an agent who knows this field. Additionally, some agents represent sellers and act as buyers themselves. So if your agent is interested in acquiring your book, this could represent a severe conflict of interests. Do your homework to ensure your agent is fully equipped to represent your sale and is entirely on your side.

Do not use a seller's agent that does not have relevant experience in the securities industry! We are too specialized to have a generalist represent you.

ATTORNEY

When it comes time to transfer ownership to your buyer, the necessary paperwork isn't hard—in fact, templates are available for download online. Nevertheless, I always recommend having a competent local attorney review your paperwork before you submit it to ensure that you're addressing your individual state's requirements.

Unfortunately, selling financial advisory practices isn't a common niche, so attorneys specializing in this area can be rare. You might find that your attorney wants to add unnecessary, tangential passages to your contract or that they're unfamiliar with major industry players and their quirks. I've been fortunate enough to develop a good working relationship with a lawyer who's well versed in the inner workings of financial advisory practices, with whom I've conducted several deals, but it took some effort for me to find him. You may end up working with two attorneys: one licensed in another state but knows this field and can write you a favorable contract, and a second who works locally and can ensure that you're meeting state requirements.

WHAT WILL THE SALES PROCESS LOOK LIKE?

YOUR ROLE IN MARKETING

In the marketing phase, your role will depend on whether you've opted to hire an agent. A professional broker usually includes marketing strategies as part of their services, but prepare for in-depth conversations about your particular book's ins and outs. Hence, the agent knows how to attract buyers. Remember in Chapter 2, when we discussed developing the "story" of your practice and what makes it shine? Whether you intend to sell your business solo or with the help of a broker, this is a great time to bring that story to the forefront.

Some firms will help you list your practice for sale on national websites, but you can expect a flood of calls if you don't have an agent. Most callers won't be qualified, but you won't know who they are, and it's unlikely you have the time or expertise to vet them yourself.

A better option is good old-fashioned networking. Get the word out. Find out which practices in your region are actively acquiring books and reach out to them. Start attending local, regional, or national conferences. Ask questions. Talk to people. Get to know other advisors at your current firm.

HOW MANY POTENTIAL BUYERS CAN YOU EXPECT?

Assuming you're planning an open-market sale—as opposed to a closed sale or succession plan—you could see dozens of interested buyers. I was recently reviewing the listing for a Pueblo, Colorado, firm—not a big moneymaker but close enough to our offices to make them a good candidate to join our team. The Pueblo book had thirty-four indications of interest from buyers all over the country. It's not uncommon to have fifty or sixty potential buyers express interest! Naturally, interest in your business will vary depending on whether you've taken the time to prepare your book, hone your "story," and identify and shore up any weak points in your business.

HOW ARE BUYERS VETTED?

When you're working with an agent, they will get dozens of calls, not you. Typically, they will ask potential buyers to fill out a detailed online profile and only consider those who complete this first. This weeds most of the wannabe financial planning moguls and leaves behind a solid profile of the remaining contenders. Many sellers' agents keep a database of prospective buyers and touch base when a new practice comes on the market.

Some prospective buyers pay a fee to get on a VIP list to get the first crack at new opportunities the seller's agent may have. VIP list members must complete a questionnaire about their practices—number of managed accounts, assets under management, certifications, team members' names, and so forth. This helps the sellers' agent to make sure there is some alignment between seller and buyer. Some questionnaires include psychographic data, such as a buyer's ties to the area and preferred type of client. For example, my questionnaire might note that I enjoy working with doctors but not engineers. My friend, on the other hand, *loves* engineers. She's assertive and plainspoken and communicates well with engineering types.

WHAT FACTORS INTO NEGOTIATIONS?

YOUR PRACTICE'S VALUATION

Some advisors might imagine that their first tool in negotiating their sale terms will be that professional valuation we discussed in Chapter 4, but they'd be wrong. Most people considering selling haven't even gotten a valuation yet. And most sellers don't generally share more than the basics of their practice until they know more about the potential buyer. Most sellers prefer to play it close to the vest. Some of that is Negotiation 101—never be the first party to put out a number—but often, it's just that the true value of a practice is a moving target. As a seller, you don't want to throw out a number only to have the stock market go bullish and make your book worth a whole lot more. In general, it's best to find the right buyer before you start negotiating the price. Also, remember that the deal you make when you sell your practice is not always as simple as a sales price. Often, there are many factors involved. For instance, you might want to sell and continue to work for the new buyer. When that happens, sales terms, salary, paid benefits, office space, and clerical help are on the bargaining block.

What's the benefit of the valuation? Sometimes it's a starting point for negotiations, and sometimes when two parties are far apart, it makes a good ending point. Ironically, during my conversations with prospective sellers, I often talk with them about how they can increase the value of their book. At one level, that doesn't make sense because I'm coaching the seller on ways they can get me to pay more for their business. However, if I am the buyer, I will get a cleaner book that is easier to integrate into my business, and that is worth paying extra. But the reality is that I want to help them improve their business, regardless of whether I buy it.

When I meet a potential seller, I don't talk business immediately. I prefer to get to know them first. I want to build trust and understanding. When the subject of price comes up, I'll ask something like, "What do you think you can get for it?" or "What kind of buyer are you looking for?" You're not selling a boat or a car on Craigslist, so take the time to get to know prospective buyers before you talk turkey.

Having a match of values between you and the buyer is critical. Make a list of your personal and professional values. Narrow it down to three to four each. You and your potential buyer should be a match for at least half of them, if not more. Do not proceed, do not pass go, and do not collect your $2 million unless your values mostly match. Without the values matching, you will have more headaches and problems, and it will not be worth it, regardless of how much money you're being offered.

Your buyer should be able to clearly articulate their values in writing. If you ask what their values are and you get the sense they are winging their answer to you, they are.

Here are our team values at Life Well Lived Financial Group:

- Live life to the fullest: We encourage team members to pursue a "life well lived" and maintain a balance between work and home. We pursue excellence in all aspects of our lives.

- Always growing: We set ambitious goals and believe if you're not spiraling up, you are falling backward.
- Continuous learning: We strive to be as knowledgeable as any team in the industry. We believe in continuous learning and sharing that knowledge with clients and peers.
- Kind and thoughtful: We work together, sharing others' burdens and valuing long-term relationships over short-term convenience.
- Service to the community: We give 1 percent of our gross revenue to causes we are passionate about and volunteer in the community. We've raised over $100,000 for our community's Empty Stocking Fund.

YOUR OBLIGATIONS

As a seller, you must ask yourself where your personal and professional values lie. For many advisors, providing for the future of their employees is a top priority. If this applies to you, be prepared to negotiate their secure jobs, proper compensation, and so forth as part of the sale. Also, consider asking the buyer to honor any outstanding commitments your business might have, such as time on an office lease.

If you're like most advisors, you'll also want to look out for the well-being of your clients, which can be tricky. Take the case of my friend Geoffrey, who found himself negotiating with a buyer who wanted only the top 20 percent of his book. This was professionally and personally distasteful for Geoff, who lived in a small town and was known by everyone. He ultimately refused the sale, telling the buyers, "These are my friends, family, and former coworkers. I have a reputation to preserve."

The issue here is that once your sale has gone through, there's very little you can do to prevent a buyer from culling unwanted clients from your book. The negotiation stage is your only chance to put your values in writing and try to ensure that all of your clients—not just the high-value ones—are ultimately cared for. In some cases, the seller has to be explicit. "This pool of clients were my former work colleagues from when I was a teacher. They may not be big clients, but I need to make sure you're going to provide service to them for at least two years," you might say. In these situations, you can add a rider to the deal that protects key clients after the transition to the buyer.

When I purchase a practice, I believe that every relationship is worth cultivating because you never know what opportunities might exist with that client. I have purchased a book, worked to develop relationships with every client over two years, and ultimately only separated from clients who failed to engage in that period.

WHAT WILL POTENTIAL BUYERS EXPECT ACCESS TO?

Interested parties will naturally be curious about your client list, but you must not share any client-specific details. Generalizations work well enough, so take the time to segment your clients by type of service, revenue per client, average client age, amount of money under management, and if relevant, career. This will enable you to describe your customers, especially top-tier clients, broadly, giving buyers a sense of whether they would be a good fit.

To use the example I mentioned earlier, you might say, "I love working with doctors but don't connect well with engineers." (This statement is true for me. Engineers tend to be highly intelligent but highly analytical; they want to figure out every dimension of a financial plan independently. This leads to a lot of online investigation that diverts them down unrelated side roads and requires a lot of reorienting, and extra work, from my end.) The good news is that any firm large enough to acquire your book will likely have a team of advisors and an associate advisor who specializes in the same customer segment you do, so your doctors—or engineers, entrepreneurs, or retirees—should be in knowledgeable hands.

Beyond a general outline of your client base, buyers will expect access to records verifying your practice's key numbers. The two most basic documents needed will show your twelve-month trailing revenue and a summary of your assets under management. Later on, the buyer is likely to want additional reports on your practice—net inflows/outflows, breakdowns by product type, growth, total financial planning fees, how much money is generating recurring revenue, number of clients, the average age of clients, average revenue per client, and so forth. It may be relevant to share the expenses you incur to run your office. These details will enable interested buyers to verify what you are saying about your practice.

A word of caution if you're planning to switch firms: your broker-dealer is watching you closely. If you suddenly start downloading a lot of practice management and data reports, your firm's artificial intelligence platform may notice the activity and conclude that you are contemplating selling. When that happens, you could get a call from someone with the company asking questions and showing a sudden interest in your future. "Hey, how are you? Just thought I'd check in and see how we can better support you!" This is good business (even though the AI aspect is a bit creepy in my book), and often it works. For example, that firm in Pueblo? The AI system flagged the seller's activity, and his home office made a successful offer to keep that advisor.

Advisors who want to give prospective buyers their reports can simply take a picture or screenshot of the documents rather than creating a fuss by downloading them. Another option is to review any needed reports over a period of time, rather than accessing them all at once.

WHAT MIGHT CAUSE BUYERS TO HIT PAUSE?

As we discussed earlier, you can run a high-performing practice and still hit a wall with buyers if the average age of your clients is too high, your business is in decline, or you've failed to establish systems to keep clients engaged. Any significant system mismatch can create a hiccup. You might approach a buyer saying, "Hey, look at our great model—we see every client once a year," only to make them hesitate because their clients expect contact three to four times per year. Such differences in company culture can make buyers think twice and should make you consider whether they're the best match for your clients.

One problem with many independent practices is that the advisor is stuck in the past, doing things as they were done twenty-five years ago. Often, the advisor is old, and their clients are seventy-five years old or older. Balances are declining as older clients withdraw their living expenses and start allocating their estate to heirs before their passing. The advisor's archaic practices and the investors' declining wealth make these books worth less than a modern, growing book, and the seller may have an inflated perception of the practice's value.

Some books are relatively young. The advisors have been in the business just a few years and don't have a lot of high-wealth clients yet. And their clients are typically on the young side, too. These books are worth less, but they may be worth acquiring if the buyer sees promise that the investors' portfolios will grow.

Find out what you can about your prospective buyer. Go to the FINRA BrokerCheck site and see if they have any major client complaints. Google their names and practice and see what comes up. Ask your peers in your community about your buyer. I once made the mistake of not checking the BrokerCheck site and found out later that the advisor had been convicted of a felony drug crime as a young man. The sale got derailed for other reasons, so nothing was lost, but I learned a valuable lesson.

KEY TAKEAWAY

Even with dozens of interested buyers, the selling process can be lengthy. Expect vetting and selection to take at least a few months, and negotiations can last just as long. Once the details have been squared away, I'd recommend budgeting at least six months to transition your clients smoothly to their new advisors and systems. This can easily become two to three years.

That said, those who properly prepare for this phase can cut down their sales time and stress by at least half. So give yourself time to prep: scope out the necessary agents or attorneys, determine what negotiation points are most important to you, and carefully segment your customer base. You'll be all the more confident when you reach that negotiating table.

Remember: If your values don't appear to align with your buyer, do not proceed!

And once that sales contract is drawn up, you can do what you do best: focus on your clients' futures. In the next chapter, we'll explore that transition process.

SALES AGREEMENT TERMS

Here are some of the terms you can expect to find in a succession or sales agreement with a buyer.

- The seller provides advance notice (usually six months) of their intent to permanently leave the financial advisory industry.
- The seller has the right to solicit third-party offers to buy the business, but the buyer has the right to match the third-party offers.
- The buyer will, in good faith, seek out financing from at least two lending institutions. If financing can't be secured, the agreement spells out the terms for the buyer to pay the seller directly (usually over a short period, such as a year).
- A "morality clause." If you commit some act that leads to the suspension or revocation of your required licenses or you're convicted of a felony, the practice purchase price is automatically reduced by 20 percent.
- Covenant not to compete and not to solicit for a period of time, typically two to three years. No soliciting the clients or helping someone else solicit the clients.
- A "clawback" provision for attrition. Here's how a typical attrition clause might be written: "If less than 90 percent of the assets attributable to the business purchased are not retained by the buyer within the first 365 days after the practice sale, then an adjustment to the purchase price shall be made, based on the following table.

PURCHASE PRICE TABLE

PERCENT OF ASSETS RETAINED	PERCENT OF DECREASE IN PURCHASE PRICE*
<90 percent or less of Assets Retained	10 percent decrease in Purchase Price
80 percent or less of Assets Retained	20 percent decrease in Purchase Price
70 percent or less of Assets Retained	30 percent decrease in Purchase Price
60 percent or less of Assets Retained	40 percent decrease in Purchase Price
50 percent or less of Assets Retained	50 percent decrease in Purchase Price
40 percent or less of Assets Retained	60 percent decrease in Purchase Price
30 percent or less of Assets Retained	70 percent decrease in Purchase Price
20 percent or less of Assets Retained	80 percent decrease in Purchase Price

*This reduction shall be deducted from the principal balance remaining on the note.

- Specify who gets paid in the event of the death of the seller. Also specify who continues to make payments in the event of the buyer's death.
- Specify what happens if, at the time of the practice sale, the buyer doesn't qualify as a successor (for example, is no longer in the industry or no longer at the same firm).

8

MAKING THE TRANSITION TO ANOTHER FIRM

WHEN CONTEMPLATING THE SALE OF YOUR BOOK, CON-
sider whether your firm signed the Protocol for Broker
Recruiting. This trade agreement, established in 2004,
allows advisors more freedom to switch firms and keep
their clients. Not all firms have entered the agreement, and
those who haven't can make things difficult for advisors
planning to sell their practice.

The agreement emerged at a time when Wall Street was
under the gun. Not only had 90 million Americans just lost
$7 trillion in the dot-com stock market collapse, but New
York Attorney General Eliot Spitzer had declared himself
"The Sheriff of Wall Street" and was working to force investment firms to make restitution to clients who had lost their
fortunes. In one case in 2003, ten firms had agreed to pay
$1.4 billion in fines for what Spitzer described as "consumer
fraud." And Spitzer indicated that case was just a warm-up;
he still had his sights leveled on firms like Merrill Lynch,

whom he claimed had encouraged customers to buy stocks that Lynch's analysts knew were terrible investments.

Spitzer's threat sent Wall Street firms scrambling to examine their practices. They were looking for any policy or practice that Spitzer might construe as criminal. One of the practices they questioned involved their approach when an advisor left the firm.

In the early 1980s and '90s, wealth management firms commonly filed injunctions that prevented departing advisors from taking their clients with them. Lawsuits were commonplace, and the legal fees were considerable. In one case, a judge threatened a firm with violations of the Economic Espionage Act because it recruited an advisor from a competing firm. Many industry leaders felt the situation had to change and that it was time to loosen the reins on their advisors.

In 2004, representatives from Morgan Stanley, Merrill Lynch, Smith Barney, and UBS created procedures for moving from one firm to another and established how much client information a departing advisor could take with them to a new firm. The agreement amounted to a "cease-fire" among major wirehouses, who were, according to one lawyer, "suing each other every Friday." If departing brokers followed the Protocol for Broker Recruiting rules, they could move around without worrying about getting sued. Soon, more than 1,700 firms nationwide joined the trade agreement, including most of the big wirehouses.

The protocol requires certain criteria to be met:

- The advisor's old and new firms must be members of the protocol.
- The advisor has to provide details about what client

information they are taking with them to their new firm. The protocol allows the advisor to keep the client's name, address, phone number, email address, and account title but can't take account statements or other personal information, such as Social Security numbers.

- An advisor's resignation must be in writing, and the new firm must ensure the advisor only contacts former clients.

More often than not, they resorted to restraining orders, cease and desist letters, and lawsuits to prevent their former employees from keeping their clients. When clients called, the old firms wouldn't reveal where their advisors went to work. Investors were trapped in the middle; their trusted advisor was suddenly gone, and no one would tell them why. Many had to wonder, *Is my money safe?* Remember the scene in *Jerry Maguire* when Jerry gets fired, and it's a frantic race between Jerry and the other sports agents to get ahold of his clients and try to keep them? This might resonate with you because you may have seen this at your firm.

The protocol eased those concerns and made transitions easier and less fraught. Soon, advisors were on the move. Morgan Stanley lost over twenty teams with more than $9 billion in assets. At the same time, many other firms roped in billions of assets when new advisors joined them. The protocol made it easier for advisors to strike out independently or join independent firms. In the seven years after the protocol was established, assets managed by independent advisors tripled to over $1.7 trillion, while assets managed by the four major wirehouse firms declined. By 2016, wirehouses employed about 47,000 advisors, while independent firms had nearly 125,000.

In 2017, the tide shifted again when Morgan Stanley, UBS, and Citibank withdrew from the broker protocol. Others have since followed. Their argument is the same one used forty years ago: they have invested heavily in technology to support their advisors, and the advisors' books would not have grown without the firm's help. That makes the advisors' clients the firm's clients. Their investments and profiles are proprietary information owned by the firm. Before long, the big firms were back in court, suing advisors who left the firm and took clients with them.

FOLLOWING PROTOCOL

Despite the 2017 departure of the big firms from the protocol, the rules are still intact and followed by around 2,000 firms in the United States.

Joining the protocol is simple. Firms need to notify the Securities Industry and Financial Markets Association that they want to join, and then they must complete a form. There's no membership cost and no formal review process for new members. Departing advisors can't take detailed client information with them, but their new firm can request account numbers and recent statements from the old firm by forwarding a client's signed authorization.

But many advisors think the rules should be loosened further. Kevin Armstrong, the chief legal officer of Docupace, a technology company providing services for financial advisors, argues that the protocol itself limits advisors' ability to achieve their fiduciary responsibilities to their clients. The wealth management industry, Armstrong says, "should move toward a modern framework that allows advisors to freely move to another firm and makes it easy for their clients to move with them." I agree wholeheartedly with his opinion.

Others point out that the world has changed enough since 2004 to make the protocol seem archaic. For one thing, the advent of social media and smartphones makes it much easier for brokers to stay in touch with their clients and makes it easy for clients to know when their broker has switched firms and how to contact them. Today's world is a far cry from what it was in 2004 when brokers needed access to the firm's database to reach their clients.

If you're considering leaving your firm, find out if your employer participates in the broker protocol. If they aren't, you're probably bound by your employment contract, and you'll need to consult an attorney about what documents you can bring to your new firm. Non-protocol firms will likely make it difficult for you to leave with your clients and join another firm. Edward Jones, for example, is a non-protocol firm. They often hire young financial advisors and train them while claiming the advisor's clients belong to the firm. Most young advisors are focused on getting established and building their book, so the non-protocol arrangement doesn't loom its ugly head until the advisor seeks more independence and realizes they are handcuffed.

There are some potential exceptions to protocol, even if you are with a protocol firm.

1. You have compensation/servicing responsibilities for specific clients with a team of advisors.
2. Sometimes, firms have a 401(k) division and funnel prospects or clients to an advisor. These don't get protocol protection.

Going after these types of clients can cause legal troubles for you.

WHAT CAN YOU COMMUNICATE TO YOUR CLIENTS?

When you are planning to sell your book and move to another firm, there are strict rules about what you can say to clients about the imminent move. You can't discuss the specifics of your move or even that you're contemplating a move. You can't tell clients when you plan to move, and you can't ask them if they would be willing to follow you if you do make a move. Often, these rules are laid out in your employment agreement. And even if the firm you are leaving and the one you are joining are members of the Protocol for Broker Recruiting, advisors are prohibited from soliciting their former clients until they have joined the new firm.

Some brokers struggle to keep their plans under wraps. The temptation to start priming the pump with their clients is too strong to resist, so they let it slip out in a phone call or a social media post. The protocol expressly forbids this. What are the penalties? You could face a lawsuit from your old firm, and state laws vary when enforcing non-compete, nonsolicitation, and nondisclosure agreements. Federal trade secret laws could also come into play. You have to be equally cautious about what you haul out of your old office: walking out with copies of confidential documents on a thumb drive could lead to an injunction and a lawsuit from your former employer and derail your plans to sell your book. You have a common-law obligation to remain loyal to your employer until you've formally left them.

Even if you are doing a protocol transition, you should consult an attorney. In many cases, the firm you are transferring to will have an attorney assigned to you and provide a number of hours of consultation time. The attorney will review your employment contract and any other agreements you've signed with your old firm. The attorney will also have an earful of advice for you to ensure you don't get yourself in trouble.

The period between your resignation letter and your final day with your old firm is called "garden leave" or "quiet period," and you probably won't be able to tell anyone—including your clients—about your imminent departure. You can't contact clients until after this period is over. For most advisors, there is no difference—resignation is immediate, and that's what I recommend.

You will want your resignation to take effect immediately. Typically, you will fax or email your resignation to your compliance person and/or your supervisor or branch manager. The resignation letter needs to be explicitly worded, and your legal counsel should help you write it. You do not need to explain why you are leaving, and you most certainly should not be critical or negative.

Once you've sent your resignation letter, you will immediately pick up the phone and call your transition person at your new firm to let them know. They will immediately begin the process of transferring your licenses from your old firm to the new firm. You will then have approximately fifteen minutes sitting quietly, in some suspense, contemplating the journey you've just started. The second your licenses have transferred, you'll get a call from the new firm. You will immediately spring into action and begin calling your clients.

Many advisors leave their offices intact when they resign to join a new firm. Cleaning out your desk and packing boxes with personal items can signal your intention to leave and potentially violate protocol rules, so it's best to keep your cards close to the vest. If you break even one minor protocol rule, you risk losing all your protections and freedom to join another firm. Your list of clients could be in jeopardy. So leave quietly and make arrangements to return after a couple of weeks to pick up your personal items.

Even when the split is somewhat amicable, disputes can erupt. If you've been at the firm for several years, your former employer might think some of the items in your office—the laptop you used, for example, or the art you hung on the wall—belongs to them. Let them have it; the costs of a legal dispute are likely to far exceed the cost of the items in dispute.

Here are some things to avoid when transitioning to a new firm. These may seem like obvious no-nos, but I bring them up because they have happened:

- Don't delete all the phone numbers in your contact management program. Some advisors do this to forestall their old firm from calling the clients to try to retain them. But that kind of stunt violates the protocols, and you could be sued.
- Don't move portfolios to cash in anticipation of your move, even if it would make the transition easier. This may not be in your client's best interest and will likely attract attention from your firm.
- Don't begin downloading client data and reports. In today's world of artificial intelligence, firms know when you suddenly and out of character start downloading reports. It's a sign that you might leave. The firm may put you and your practice under heightened supervi-

sion behind the scenes. Some advisors get around this by using the phone to take pictures of the files as they appear on their computer screens.

- In the run-up to your departure, don't schedule a rash of appointments with clients in the period immediately after you leave. This is perceived as a sign of bad faith. Just call your clients if you want to alert them to what's happening. Regularly scheduled meetings are okay to continue to hold. We see many advisors who book their entire year of appointments up front. It's okay to hold these.

- Don't stop/change client payouts before you leave to make it easier to keep payouts on track. This is not in the client's interest and opens you up to legal issues.

- Don't delete client files, notes, documents, statement copies, and so forth. Don't delete a form you created, such as a financial plan template. This may be tempting—after all, you created it; why leave it behind for someone else to use—but it's a red flag.

- Don't talk to ANYONE about your plans except those who need to know. Your spouse. Maybe a trusted member of your team. Loose lips sink ships and transition plans.

A couple of things to make sure to do:

- Help your clients take their required minimum distributions (RMDs) from their IRAs. You likely have a nice report from your firm that shows the amount each client needs to take from their IRA. When you leave, you will not have the exact dollar amounts. You can manually calculate the RMD, but you'll need a year-end IRA account balance. You won't have access to your client statements anymore, so you won't have that number. Get the RMDs taken so you don't have an extra headache to tackle. And do not take the RMD report from your old firm with you.

I learned firsthand what happens when you reveal your transition plans to others. Remember Ed from the case study in Chapter 6? While trying to lure him away from his big bank, we felt everything was on track when he called in a panic. His bank boss had called and told him, "I know you're planning to leave. We're not going to make it easy for you if you do. However, give us a chance to come up with solutions to your problems. Give us a chance to find a good successor within our firm for you."

We had a long discussion about how his boss found out.

"Did you download a bunch of your practice reports to a thumb drive?"

"Absolutely not. And the only person I told was my assistant, who is moving with me, and one advisor in another city with whom I have a close relationship. Not a chance they spilled the beans. Did *you* tell anyone?"

Well, I had told an advisor with my firm but asked him not to share the news with anyone.

The next time I was in his office, his administrative assistant asked, "When will Ed be joining?" Later that day, I talked to another advisor in the office who said, "I understand you recruited Ed! I used to work with him."

I never learned who spilled the beans to Ed's boss, but the "loose lips" nearly killed a $100 million deal for my team. Ed stayed with the bank for almost a year before we resumed serious talks about his transition. Eventually, he did, but it would have happened much sooner if we'd been able to keep a lid on the deal.

GET ON THE HORN

Once your licenses have been transferred to the new firm, you need to get on the phone. I would create a phone script for client calls that highlight the advantages of the move and explain how things will continue to work as they always have, with regular portfolio reviews and direct access to the advisor and their staff. Some make videos that they post to their websites, and others write letters of assurance and explanation. The key is to make a case for why the move is in everyone's interest while avoiding direct criticism of your former employer.

Work with your current firm to get preapproval on your client correspondence. These communications are considered sales literature by the Financial Industry Regulatory Authority (FINRA). You must have it preapproved if you send it to more than twenty-five people. The firm will likely have a bland, rather generic preapproved letter that is probably good enough. You're busy enough; don't waste your time trying to write your own.

Even in amicable or undisputed splits, departing advisors should expect to lose some clients. The attrition rate varies but usually is between 10 percent and 20 percent. Advisors who've kept in close contact with their clients and provided proactive advice can keep their attrition rate to 5 percent or less. Advisors who haven't systematically kept in touch with their clients may lose 20–25 percent. During the COVID-19 pandemic, any advisor dramatically ramped up their client contact. Those advisors who later transitioned to a new firm had dramatically better results, and it isn't uncommon for advisors to transition MORE assets to the new firm than they had before at the old firm. If your sales contract is like most, your negotiated price will be based on a 5 percent attrition rate, no more. If you pass that mark, the attrition clause kicks in, and the difference in revenue is deducted from your purchase revenue to protect the buyer.

So if you want to keep that attrition figure low—and we all do—you can begin by brainstorming how to ease clients into the forthcoming sale. Your approach here will vary widely depending on one particular factor: whether your sale is external or internal.

EXTERNAL SALE

Even though you can't communicate your plans before the sale, that doesn't mean you can't plot how that communication will unfold. So take the time to hammer out those details. Develop a specific, step-by-step strategy, then organize your files, clients, and time of departure to facilitate that plan. A crucial part of your strategy—and of reducing the risk of attrition—will be to reach out to clients individually to explain the change. Make sure you've correctly segmented your clients by service type and investment, then organize this segmentation into a list from highest- to lowest-value customers. This will form the basis of your client call list, a tool that will come in handy very soon.

Your new firm will likely have a proven process for your transition. Follow it! You may not have done this before, but they have done it many times. Don't assume you have "a better way."

So how might such a communication strategy play out? Picture this: It's noon on Friday, the beginning of a long weekend. The minute after your employment ends, you send out a prepared email blast informing clients of the sale. You let them know to look out for the transfer paperwork, which will be overnighted and should arrive Saturday morning.

Meanwhile, once your license transfers—which should take only about fifteen minutes—it's time to jump on the phone and start calling clients individually, beginning with those high-value customers. I would start with a few "gimmes"—those clients who love you—so you can get your sea legs. Explain that you've decided to move your book to a new firm, how that move benefits them specifically, and why you've made this choice. (Give only positive reasons—don't knock the outgoing firm. Nobody likes to hear that negativity. And it could set you up for legal troubles with the old firm.) Reiterate that a transfer packet is headed their way and assure them that the paperwork won't be onerous: "All I need you to do is fill out a few blanks—your account numbers, date of birth, that kind of thing. Then you can either have UPS send it back or input your information into the new firm's secure website." Tell them they can call you directly if they have questions about the process.

The process isn't nearly as demanding as it used to be. With most firms, the client can input their accounts and account numbers online. The receiving firm should have a team at their home office that creates the transfer paperwork. It's then sent to the client for e-signatures. Advisors who switched firms as recently as four years ago tell horror stories about processing thousands of documents, staying up all night, printing and stapling forms, and licking envelopes to mail to clients.

From there, it's just a matter of continuing down your list—again, working from highest- to lowest-value customer. Surprisingly, some advisors approach this process willy-nilly, starting at the top of the alphabet and working their way down. But this means some of their highest-value clients don't get a call for hours or days after receiving that initial email. This is a lot of time to pass while that client wonders exactly what's being done with their financial future. It also gives your former firm time to convince them to stay with your old firm.

In my experience, with a lot of coffee and a little determination, you will have made it to the bottom of that list by the end of the weekend. And good for you, because every client deserves to feel the personal touch of your attention. Time is of the essence! Do not assume your clients don't want to hear from you over the weekend or in the evening. You must call them, and even though you may only leave a message, they need to hear from you first, not from some advisor at the old firm.

WHAT IF YOU'RE AT A NON-PROTOCOL FIRM?

You may be leaving a non-protocol firm. In this case, you cannot take any client data or solicit clients. In most states, you can announce your departure and respond to client questions.

Before you leave your non-protocol firm, remember you still have a duty of loyalty to your current employer. If you signed a confidentiality or nonsolicitation agreement, you can typically expect your non-protocol firm to enforce it through legal action if necessary. The degree of enforceability is highly dependent on state laws. You may have signed a non-compete agreement, but these are difficult to enforce in most states.

In general, transitioning advisors can contact their clients as long as they aren't using data taken from the firm. But they can't solicit them. This is a fine line.

As you can see, it can get complicated. You need to make sure you consult with an attorney and get guidance to make sure you stay out of trouble.

INTERNAL SALE

In some ways, guiding clients through an internal sale is similar to that of an external sale—it can just happen a lot more gradually.

I've been surprised over the years by how many clients have reached out to say, "You're in your fifties now; you're not going to work forever. What's your plan?" Or even, "Who's taking over for you? If something happens, we don't want to be abandoned." Unlike in an external sale, it's perfectly legal and smart to inform clients of a forthcoming internal sale. In many cases, the advisors who will one day take over your book work just down the hallway, so do everyone a favor and start introducing your successors as soon as your sales plans are in motion. People hate change but hate it less when it's slow and steady.

As you near the actual date of sale, I'd once again recommend sending out an email blast reminding clients of your coming resignation, then calling them individually to explain the change. Reassure each that you will guide the process yourself or with others within your firm. And if you want to reduce attrition, invite your high-value clients to face-to-face meetings with you and the advisor taking over their portfolio. This allows you to show clients how competent and kind their new advisors will be, smoothing the eventual transition into their care. Advisors who take these steps and keep the client's peace of mind as their goal find that relationships are kept intact, retention is terrific, and the value of their books is preserved.

HOW ELSE CAN I DECREASE ATTRITION RATES?

Once a sale is complete, the most effective method of retaining clients I've seen is to integrate yourself, at least temporarily, with the new firm. Use the new team's branding. Change your system to match theirs. Use the same investment portfolios and follow the new firm's client service model. Even if you're staying for only a short time, doing this will make the transition easier for your clients, reduce attrition, and increase your practice's value.

This approach works exceptionally well if you plan to work for a few more years before retiring. Your clients trust you, so your job now is to use that trust to build a bridge between clients and their new team. Showcase each team member, familiarize clients with new support staff and office managers, and introduce fellow advisors to your client processes. By the time you exit the firm, your clients' trust in their new advisory team should be secure.

When making an external sale, insist that the new firm assign someone to be a transition expert to shepherd clients and their paperwork through. For example, during a recent acquisition, my colleague Joe parked himself in the transitioning advisor's office for six weeks and made himself available to incoming clients. He would field questions, scan documents, push through paperwork, and do anything that would help them transition with minimal disruption to their everyday lives. Your transition guru can either be someone from your own office, like Joe, or a professional borrowed from another practice, but they should be a licensed advisor or staff person familiar with all the moving pieces of your specific transition. Sometimes the receiving firm will assign a person from their home office to be physically in your office helping you, if your practice is big enough.

I think every firm during a transition will provide "virtual help"—someone you can reach by phone or video chat. Beware, though. We recently heard of a transitioning advisor who had been promised a "new advisor support team" to help him with technology, tools, and paperwork. It sounded great, but the support team was in a different time zone. While working in the evenings, he couldn't pick up the phone and get support after 4:00 p.m.! So his plan to call clients during the day and learn processes during the evening didn't work.

WHAT OTHER DETAILS SHOULD I KEEP IN MIND?

Here's the good news: with all the effort a transition requires, at least the paperwork is easy.

I recently did a transition demo for a seller in Denver. This advisor was anticipating I'd walk him through a mountain of paperwork, but that wasn't the case. As we discussed above, at the time of sale, your clients will receive a small packet of documents with simple blanks to fill in—such as their account number, beneficiaries, and income—and then return. Clients can then review the final version online and e-sign. And that's it!

Some advisors leaving one firm for another in anticipation of selling their book may have to repay a signing or retention bonus. Brokerage firms will claw back any payment if the advisor leaves before the agreed-upon term, which may be as long as five to seven years. Unless you move from one protocol firm to another, they can prevent you from soliciting clients at your new firm. You can try to get out of repaying those funds by arguing that your old firm didn't live up to its promises, but arbitration panels usually find in favor of the firm.

KEY TAKEAWAY

Leaving a firm or transitioning to a new one is not as complicated or acrimonious as it used to be. Still, you must follow some essential rules to avoid conflict. Ensure you don't violate the Protocol for Broker Recruiting requirements, and keep your plans to leave or sell private until the time is right. Draw up a plan for quickly communicating your move to your clients. Although some attrition is likely, communicating clearly with your clients can dramatically reduce the number of lost clients.

9

WELCOME TO RETIREMENT

ONE OF THE FIRST PRACTICES I EVER ACQUIRED BELONGED to an advisor in a small, rural Colorado town. This advisor—we'll call him Tom—was essential during our transition, briefing us on the needs and quirks of each client and helping those clients feel comfortable under the shade of our umbrella.

But once the transition was over? Tom went MIA—in the best possible way.

My partners and I would arrange to meet him for lunch, then push for more advice on his former clients: "I met with Lizzie and Bob about their annuities the other day, and they were unhappy. I just don't know how to handle them yet. What can you tell me?" But although Tom was happy to chat about anything else under the sun, business was simply off the table. He deflected our questions every time, providing only generic advice and feedback.

It was frustrating as hell from our end. But I've rarely seen such a healthy approach to retirement. He understood that his continued involvement with clients would confuse them and that he might indirectly encourage them to keep seeking his advice. He didn't want to sabotage the efforts of the new advisor, so he made a clean break.

We've had retired sellers call our office regularly to check in on their former clients, making us their entertainment on a dull afternoon. Others call to complain that their clients are unhappy and that we need to take better care of them. But Tom? The moment he left the advisory world, he let all that fly like a balloon into the atmosphere.

What's the difference between Tom and so many other retired advisors? Most of us sell to get away from something, but Tom was running toward something. He had a plan: he wanted to play golf every day of the year, and he wasn't about to let business bog him down.

So what can we learn from Tom? Three lessons: Do your best during the transition, but don't let your job define you or your life. Once you leave your profession, leave it; don't try and cling to what's behind you. And finally, practice what you've preached for so long: have a vision of your retirement future, and structure your life and finances to support that vision.

TREAT THE TRANSITION PERIOD LIKE YOUR JOB

When transitioning control to your successors, I have two pieces of advice: Do your job well, then get out.

In the last chapter, we outlined several steps to reduce the risk of client attrition. But in all likelihood, your role in keeping clients aboard won't stop immediately with the sale of your book. Even if you enter retirement directly, rather than working under the buyers for a few years, it's a good idea to keep in touch with them and answer any questions they might have—at least until the transition period is complete.

For example, I like to meet with advisors whose books I've purchased at least monthly for the first six months following the sale. I might want to ask, "What's the easiest way to deal with the Johnsons?" or perhaps, "I see you never put [this particular product] into place with Bill Krasinski. Why not?" After about six months, we switch to meeting every other month or once a quarter.

Your retirement doesn't mean your relationships with clients simply evaporate. It's not uncommon for people to reach out to their former advisors for, well, advice. You might hear, "This guy you sent me to? He's rescheduled me twice and isn't returning my calls. What am I supposed to do?" Or even, "What this new advisor is telling me flies in the face of what you told me. Now she wants me to switch to this new product instead. What's she even talking about?"

If you have ongoing friendships with some clients after you retire, cut off dialogue about the new advisor. It's just going to frustrate you, and with extra time on your hands, you may find yourself wrapped up in (and perhaps enjoying) the drama. Just say no. Deflect the conversation and change the subject. Feel free to pass along what the client said to the new advisor, but don't take sides. You probably don't even want to hear the new advisor's side of the story; again, it's just more drama you don't need.

As we also discussed in the last chapter, your clients trust you more than their new advisors, so use this transition time to keep building bridges between the two. For example, shortly after acquiring a high-value client, I reviewed his files and decided that a younger advisor at our office would suit his needs perfectly. I brought this advisor to meetings and allowed him to conduct the follow-up, thinking all was well. But it soon got back to me that this client had contacted the seller—his retired former advisor—to complain. Since my younger colleague's name wasn't on the front door, our new client thought he was being handed off to the B team. Of course, my colleague isn't second string at all—he's more knowledgeable than I am—but our new client had no way of knowing that.

In a situation like this, you, as the trusted former advisor, can aid the transition by making micro-adjustments to clients' perceptions. I could reassure my new client of my colleague's competence all day. But wouldn't that argument be much more compelling from the credible, reliable advisor he already knows?

In my case, I talked with the former advisor and explained that the advisor I was bringing in had more experience with business-owner issues than I did. Moreover, he was a Certified Financial Planner™ with eighteen years of experience. The selling advisor agreed with me and later chatted with the client, reassuring him that he was in good hands. My younger colleague has had a productive relationship with the client for several years.

You might not feel like fielding questions from either the buyer or seller but for the good of your former clients—and to ensure that you don't activate that dreaded attrition clause—it's a good idea to keep that dialogue going for six to twelve months.

BUT ALSO, DON'T LET THE TRANSITION *BECOME* YOUR JOB

No one expects you to remain plugged into your old firm indefinitely, and you shouldn't expect this either. I courted one particular advisor who ultimately agreed to sell to me. After the sale, we met monthly until the clients began to settle in, at which point we switched to quarterly. Over time, we had less and less to talk about: the clients were fine, and I didn't want to waste his time with unnecessary meetings and questions. Little did I know that my reduction in attention had offended him. He later told me, "You know, I thought we would continue to be friends. I know you're busy, but I'm sorry not to hear from you anymore."

As a buyer, it was never my goal to make the seller feel undervalued or disrespected. Recognizing and respecting the seller's perspective is a skill I can certainly work on. But as a seller, remember that your part in this transition will eventually end, and this is a good thing for you and the client. So instead of fighting the end of your transition, embrace it and accept the opportunity to release all that stress and strain.

ONCE YOU'RE OUT OF THE GAME, *STAY* OUT OF THE GAME

This one is tricky. Once you've spent decades dispensing expert financial advice, it becomes second nature to answer whatever questions come your way—and people will certainly give you opportunities. A former client might approach you at the grocery store and say, "Hey, I've heard about [this new product]. What do you think I should do?" And you might think, Oh, I'm not really acting as an advisor, just helping out a friend. But now that you've retired, you must train yourself to resist temptation. Not only are you no longer licensed, but the rules and practices of this field can also change so fast that your advice might no longer be relevant or helpful.

A client of mine recently contacted me after experiencing this scenario. A retired advisor had told him to consider a particular strategy that my client now wanted to try out. I immediately felt uncomfortable because this advice was sorely out of date, and the last thing I wanted to do was make a fellow advisor look bad. Unfortunately, I was forced to explain, "No, I don't think that's a great strategy anymore. That's not appropriate for your situation." As a former advisor, you know better than anyone how quickly this game changes. So let retirement be your opportunity to step off the field and let someone else coach. Not only will this protect the changing interests of your former clients, but it will also protect your legacy as a talented and insightful advisor.

Additionally, letting your exit really be your exit could mean preserving your feelings. I've seen this situation unfold. Say you've got a family you've served for years, first the parents and then the adult children. After your retirement, you discover those children abandoned their new firm within months or even weeks of the sale. So you give the buyer an angry phone call and demand to know what mistake they've made to force out such well-served clients.

Then your buyer throws you a curveball. The younger clients only stuck with your firm for so long out of a sense of duty. You helped their parents through retirement, after all. It just wouldn't be right to leave—that is, until you retired, giving them an opening to search for a better fit.

So once you're out, stay out and keep that ego in check.

BE SMART WITH YOUR FINANCES

Almost every time I've purchased an advisor's practice and paid them a fat stack of cash, they are soon driving around in a new SUV. This strikes me as incredibly ironic. After all, they've spent their entire careers helping people manage their money well. But I've found that their reasoning generally comes from one of two places. They want to show off their success—I was a financial advisor! Look how well I did!—or they don't know what to do with that significant influx of money.

The sale of your business will probably be the most significant financial asset you'll ever have, so I'd hope you'd be smart enough to do what your clients once did: get a financial advisor.

Some of you might rail against this idea. After all, you're already an expert, right? But before you shut the book on me, remember two important things: First, you are not and cannot be objective regarding your own money. That's just human nature. And second, let me emphasize again that you know how quickly this market can shift and how fast your knowledge can become obsolete. Look at how often tax laws change or the recent sharp rise in inflation rates. These things can change on a dime. Do you want them messing up your future?

So plan for that future. Rather than wasting your new-found wealth on an impulse-buy BMW, map out where you want that money to go. Do you want to hit golf balls all day like Tom? Downsize to a house on the beach? Travel the world? Whatever your ideal retirement, visualize it, share that vision with a talented advisor—surely you know one or two—and let them help turn your vision into reality.

Here's an interesting fact. You probably have a bucket

list of things you want to do during retirement. On average, people complete their retirement bucket list in the first 36 months after they quit working! You need to find meaning and purpose beyond your bucket list. If you don't, your retirement signals the universe to get the nursing home bed and the coffin ready for you.

You need to be psychologically ready for retirement, not just financially ready. There's a great TED Talk to look up featuring Dr. Riley Moynes, who talks about the four phases of retirement.

The first stage is the vacation phase. You do what you want, wake up when you want, and have no set routine. This stage lasts about a year, then loses its luster. You begin to miss the routine, get bored, and start thinking, "Is this all there is?"

The second phase is feeling lost. You've lost your routine, sense of identity, relationships, purpose, and even power. This is where you see the three Ds—divorce, depression, and decline, both physical and mental. You experience fear and anxiety.

The third phase is trial and error. You explore how to make your life meaningful again. How can I contribute? This is a time of hope but also disappointment and failure, as you may get involved in things that don't work out. You may even find yourself slipping back into the second phase.

Not everyone makes it to the fourth phase of reinventing yourself and your role, but those who do are often the happiest people you will ever meet. They have reinvented and rewired. They answered the questions "What is my purpose?" and "How do I make the most of my retirement?" Almost always, this involves service to others.

KEY TAKEAWAY

It's time to take the advice you've been giving others all these years. Protect your money, leave your professional days behind you where they belong, and approach your retirement with intention. My wise friend Tom is winning at retirement because he took these steps. He put his business into competent hands, then sailed off into the sunset when the moment was right and never looked back.

Do yourself a favor and try your best to do the same.

CONCLUSION

A CHINESE PROVERB SAYS, "THE BEST TIME TO PLANT A tree is twenty years ago." When I read that recently, I chuckled and thought, "Well, the best time to start preparing to sell your practice is at least five years ago!" The second best time is today.

If you're a financial advisor starting to think about retirement, you should begin taking steps now to prepare for that event. Ask yourself a few key questions:

- **Am I ready to retire?** Is my business still growing, or has it already reached its peak and started to decline? Am I meeting regularly with clients and planning with them, or am I coasting and letting things slide because I'm comfortable with my income? Please, please, please! Don't make the mistake of coasting on your income while not adequately serving your clients just because it's easy. You are doing your clients a major disservice, and in many cases, you are hurting them. Are my clients reaching the age where their portfolios will start shrinking as they draw on them for retirement? If I continue working, do I want to be able to cut back my hours slowly?

- **How much is my practice worth?** I've heard you can get two to three times recurring revenue. If so, is that enough for me to retire? Get a valuation.
- **What can I do right now to improve the value of my book?** How can I increase my percentage of affluent clients and transition my more basic clients to a model that better suits their needs? How can I transition more of my clients to managed accounts and out of the world of up-front commissions, which won't help me get more for my practice when I attempt to sell it? Are there clients I should hand off to someone else because they are hurting my practice value?
- **How easy will it be for me to sell?** Is my staff the right size for this practice? Do I have an affordable lease and reasonable overhead for servicing my clients? Do I have a continuity plan so someone can step in and keep the operation running smoothly? What do I need to change about my current practice to ensure that? How much time will I need to prepare my practice for sale—a year? Two years? Five?
- **What is the story of my practice?** What can I tell prospective buyers about why I got into this business? What philosophy have I followed to provide outstanding service to my clients? What makes my practice stand out and makes it worth acquiring?
- **What do I envision happening with my practice?** Should I merge with another firm and arrange to have them take over my book? Should I just sell it on the open market? What about bringing on a family member or an associate? If so, who? How much time will they need to get up to speed? How good a teacher am I?

- **How can I ensure my clients get great service and sound advice?** The last thing I want is to get in line at Safeway and hear one of my former clients complain about the person I chose to handle their investments. How do I make sure I pick the right person or outfit so that doesn't happen?
- **What are my values, and how do I ensure they align with any potential buyer?**

THE RIGHT TIME

I've tried to encourage you in this book to patiently choose the right retirement path for you and your clients. I also want to remind you that most financial advisors hang on too long. They allow their skills to rust and their client service to decline. Many lose up to a third of their practice's value by waiting too long to sell. Or worse, they run their practice into the ground and close their doors.

My goal in writing this book is to help you understand your options. Whether you decide to sell externally, internally, or not at all, I hope this book has made the choices clear to you.

I hope I've also allayed any apprehensions you have about the process of selling. Although the financial advising business is still a fairly new industry, there are established practices that make valuing and selling these practices straightforward. Buyers like my team and me have lots of data from previous sales in various markets to fully understand the metrics that drive the price of an advising practice. Although every practice is different, determining the value of someone's book doesn't require much guesswork. This robust dataset and industry-accepted approaches to selling should reassure you by taking the uncertainty and risk out of the process.

When it comes to financial planning practices, it is currently a seller's market. There are buyers out there eager to talk to you about acquiring your book. They are paying top dollar, and they are willing to help you transition into retirement. This puts you in the catbird seat, with many great options to consider. This book should help you sort through those options and find the one that's right for you.

CONTINUING YOUR LEGACY

As you consider those options, take the time you need to get to know your potential buyers. No one knows your clients better than you, so look for the person who will continue your legacy. This may take some time. Don't rush the process. Meet with potential suitors and get to know them. Find out how they work and what their values are.

Just as you have options for whom to sell to, you also have options for how you want to get paid. Some of you will want to continue working for a few years, perhaps at a slowly declining commitment level, and some of you are eager to make a clean break and move on to the next thing. Either of these options is available to you and entirely up to you. In a seller's market, it's much easier to dictate your terms or transition. Use this book to understand those options better.

Whatever you decide to do, follow the wise advice you've given your clients over the years. Retire *to* something rather than retiring *from* something. Think about how you want to spend your time in retirement and take steps to achieve that ideal. More golf? More volunteer work? More time with the grandkids? As you work toward selling your practice, think about those options and let your anticipation build. Plan for the financial adjustments that retirement typically calls for. Use these thoughts as motivation while you work toward getting your book ready to sell.

If you're among the estimated 60 percent of retirement-age financial advisors who have yet to identify a successor for their practice, it's time to get a plan. Start getting annual valuations of your practice. Act on the opportunities your valuation will identify and use the yearly valuation to measure your progress. Develop a continuity plan and get an emergency transition set up.

The worst thing you can do is to let your practice slide. Most advisors don't realize the value of retiring when their practice is at its peak. Find out if you've reached that peak, and then ask yourself, "Can I go higher? Or am I sliding down from the mountaintop?" If you're in doubt, reach out to a colleague and ask for their honest opinion. If you need an impartial opinion, feel free to contact me at paulinthesprings@yahoo.com or at (719) 440-2878. I'm happy to answer questions or provide general feedback on your situation. Perhaps I can add some value to your situation and steer you in the right direction. Even though you may not be ready for retirement, your clients might be ready for you to hand the keys to a younger advisor with fresh ideas and enthusiasm. Just as you've earned their trust over the years by carefully managing their money, they now deserve the same loyalty they've shown you. Do what's right for them, just as you've always done.

ACKNOWLEDGMENTS

THANK YOU TO MY TEAM AT LIFE WELL LIVED FINANCIAL Group. Our Integrator, Roberta Daugherty, is the rock of the business and keeps everything running smoothly while I work on what I love to do: go out and talk to advisors. Joe Strike, our Head of Practice Transitions, is an encyclopedia of industry knowledge and has a gift for quickly putting a deal together and cutting through the BS. He is our concierge as we transition clients to our team. Kimberly Cavaliere, our Director of Operations, ensures our clients feel the love and receive great service. Without these folks, we would never have developed our expertise in advisor successions. Thanks to all who read and reviewed this book, ensured it made sense, and kept my worst ideas in check. Finally, thanks to my wife and best friend, Sharon Butts, the much-needed stabilizer in my life who keeps me grounded in reality when my instinct is to be a dreamer.

I am eternally grateful to my wife, Sharon. She is the catalyst for me reaching for higher heights than I thought possible. My career transformed when we got married.

Thank you to my two partners, Roberta Daugherty and

Joseph Strike, for believing in me and giving me my space to do what I do best.

And a special thanks to Advisor Legacy, a company that specializes in mergers and acquisitions for financial advisors. I've learned so much from them, and they've been a great partner in so many ways. I highly recommend them for any practice purchase and sale transaction. www.advisorlegacy.com.

ABOUT THE AUTHOR

PAUL FRANCO has been a financial advisor for nearly thirty years. His firm, Life Well Lived Financial Group, has three locations in the Front Range of Colorado. He and his team have completed multiple practice and advisor transitions.

Paul divides his time between Colorado Springs and Gunnison, Colorado. He earned his BA from Western Colorado University and his MBA from the University of Colorado. He is a Certified Financial Planner™, Chartered Financial Consultant®, BFA Behavioral Finance Advisor, and an APMA Accredited Portfolio Management Advisor. In his free time, he enjoys skiing, hiking, running, fishing, drinking beer, eating good food, and traveling.

www.ingramcontent.com/pod-product-compliance
Lightning Source LLC
Chambersburg PA
CBHW031857200326
41597CB00012B/449